The Rider's Edge

OVERCOMING
THE PSYCHOLOGICAL
CHALLENGES OF RIDING

THE RIDER'S EDGE

By Janet Sasson Edgette and the Editors of Practical Horseman

Printed in the USA.

First Published in 2004 by PRIMEDIA Equine Network
656 Quince Orchard Road, #600
Gaithersburg, MD 20878
301-977-3900
VP, Group Publishing Director: Susan Harding
Director, Product Marketing: Julie Beaulieu
Editorial Director: Cathy Laws

Order by calling 800-957-5813 or online at www.TheEquineCollection.com

Practical Horseman
PO Box 589, Unionville, PA 19375
Editor: Mandy Lorraine
Articles Editor: Deborah Lyons
Editorial/Production Coordinator: Susan E. Simone

Book Design: Lauryl Suire Eddlemon
Illustrations: Cindy Revell

Library of Congress Cataloging-in-Publication Data

Edgette, Janet Sasson.
The rider's edge : overcoming the psychological challenges of riding / by Janet
Sasson Edgette and the Editors of Practical Horseman.
p. cm.
ISBN 1-929164-22-X
1. Horsemanship--Psychological aspects. I. Practical Horseman. II. Title.
SF309.E316 2004
798.2'3--dc22
2004003201

For my boys:
John, Casey, Austin, and Jake—
whose kindness, generosity, and
enthusiasm for another's dream speak
volumes about the type of men they are.

INTRODUCTION

O
f all my different articles, books, and essays, the writings in this collection are among my very favorites. They were first featured monthly in *Practical Horseman* magazine, in a sport-psychology column (originally called "e-mail" and later on "Heads Up") between the years of 1995 and 2003. Readers wrote in with questions, and I wrote back with answers. Sometimes I told stories about riders I'd known or helped who had resolved similar dilemmas. Other stories were my own, telling about my experiences trying to juggle riding and working and family, as well as manage the mix of intense hungers and jubilations and frustrations that come right at you in this compelling sport.

Riders and trainers often assume that equestrian sport psychology concerns itself only with performance nerves. They overlook many of the other issues this sport can bring up that can't be remedied by a new bit, a new horse, or extra lessons. The issues include a rider's fear of ruining a new horse or of getting injured, rebuilding confidence after a bad fall, sportsmanship, trainer-rider relationships, finally finding but then losing a good horse, and dealing with training setbacks. They also include figuring out how to balance a sport as time-intensive as riding with making a living or building a career, raising children, caring for family members, or making time for the other important people in a rider's life who can be left wondering where they fit into the mix. Riding is not a simple activity.

But it is one that challenges us in ways few other activities or sports (or even people) do. No matter how hard a rider tries, she can never disguise her true self from the horses she partners. Perfectionism, anxiety, bullishness, impatience, or penchants for control all come out in the rider-horse relationship. To make it worse, they come out in full view of trainers, friends, judges, and family. But so does the good stuff—horses and observers alike will recognize the kind rider, the patient rider, the definitive but diplomatic rider. Anybody trying to "fake" the good ride eventually just winds up in a vortex of tension and ill humor—and deteriorating performance.

For too long, performance coaches and sport psychologists have tried to help their clients by getting them to change, or at least to believe they have changed, how they feel or think; thus their focus on relaxing, self-affirmation, ejecting negative thoughts, and the like. This doesn't make sense to me. I think it dehumanizes the person who's taught to believe her reactions to events are dismissible. They aren't. However, neither are they the problem she thinks they are. Fears, performance anxieties, and peculiar thoughts become problems only when a person believes she shouldn't be having them, or that they are stupid, or that she will ride more effectively only when they go away. None of those is true. By learning to ride well in spite of feeling nervous or of thinking ugly thoughts, and by compensating for how those feelings or thoughts affect her riding, a rider is liberated from the conundrum of trying to exert control over something that can be "controlled"—but at enormous expense: The rider who contrives a psychological state of being cannot afford to really know herself or her sport.

This has been the fundamental philosophy behind all my work as an equestrian sport psychologist. It is widely applicable, and it's practical without being hokey. For me, it transcends sport and riding; it's as much a part of my philosophies about general psychology, parenting, and living everyday life. I think of it also as having soul—a quality missing in all the performance-enhancement gimmicks imposed on people who think they need to be freed of what are really just bewildering, but normal and predictable, 'symptoms' of being a human being.

Janet Sasson Edgette
Chester Springs, Pennsylvania

CONTENTS

FOREWORD

By George H. Morris

Fifty years ago my great riding instructor, Gordon Wright, taught us about fears: physical fear, or the fear of getting hurt; mental fear, the fear of making a mistake. According to Gordon, one had to go very slow teaching people with physical fear so as never, never to over-face them. Of course, some of us younger, non-daring types he'd challenge by saying, *"What do you want to do, live forever!?!"* And of course, gritting our teeth, we'd head down to the crossrail we'd jumped a thousand times, except this time he'd placed a pair of five-foot-high sheep-hurdle wings behind it. (And on a green horse to boot!)

As far as mental fear was concerned, he had a phrase for that, too: *"What are you trying to be, a god-damn perfectionist!?! Get on with it!"* Of course, Gordon Wright, being the great personality and horseman that he was, and being a cavalry officer, intuitively knew how to get rid of fears. Facing you with them in small acceptable doses, much like inoculations, he made you immune to your fear. Working according to the individual, he would physically and mentally toughen you up.

Gordon talked about "stage fright" (mental fear). He told me my "stage fright" moved me up, which it did. Other riders it caused to freeze. Gordon also told me I had to be part psychiatrist to be a good teacher. And of course he was right. Actually I've never met a communicator, a teacher like Gordon Wright. He was always way ahead of his time. And here was a door he opened, which now we have walked through—sport psychology.

Sport psychology is now a subject, a specialty, all to itself. It doesn't necessarily deal with the techniques associated with riding or training horses, but rather with the rider's mind. (And indirectly with the horse's mind.)

We have evolved to that point today as human beings, athletes, riders. The crux of our successes or failures lies in the mind. The Germans win so many medals in equestrian sport not so much because of their methodology but because of their "nerves."

I have known Janet Edgette for years now as a friend, as a riding pupil, and as a sport psychologist. She is a lovely, intelligent, and attractive person. In all three compartments she excels. She is an accomplished horsewoman. And is she ever dedicated to her profession.

Janet is the guru of sport psychology in equestrian sport. Of course her words of wisdom are guaranteed to help athletes of any sport, as well as people just trying to get through life. Janet has reached that wonderful stage in her career when she can call on practical experience, having dealt with almost every conceivable problem, as well as her wealth of theoretical knowledge.

Like all of Janet's works, this one you won't want to miss. Read it, enjoy it, savor it, digest it, and I guarantee your game of riding as well as your game of life will improve.

George H. Morris

[CHAPTER 1]

Dealing with
Show and
Performance
Nerves

WHY I DON'T TEACH RELAXATION

THE CALL

A dad phones, worried about his daughter. He's spent several weeks standing helplessly by, watching Liz shake and jitter and hyperventilate on the eve of her equitation classes. She always goes on to place well, but then she needs three days to settle her somersaulting stomach. Dad wants Liz to feel more confident and less nervous. Could I teach her some relaxation techniques or something?

THE CONSULT

I meet with Liz and her dad and learn that she worries a lot—about how many classes to enter at each show, about disappointing her trainer and parents, and about doing at least as well as she did the last time she competed—which, because she usually does very well, means she has to do very well or better than very well (!?) every time she goes out. I was beginning to understand why Liz spent her pre-show days all aquiver.

Did Liz's dad know why his daughter was always raising the bar on herself? "No," he replied, sadly. "Her mom and I have been trying to help Liz to appreciate her efforts more than her placings. We tell her just to do the best she can, and that we love most seeing her enjoy riding. Isn't there some kind of technique she can learn to relax?"

Relax?, I think to myself. Relaxing to a tape at home the evening before a show isn't going to help this kid manage what's going on in her mind the next day.

"It's really not about relaxing," I begin to explain. "Liz doesn't need to learn how to relax. She needs to learn how to problem-solve about her show program, and how to let 'good' be good enough. She's nervous as all heck because she demands the world and then some from herself."

SPORT PSYCH ISN'T RELAXATION!

Sport psychology has been yoked to relaxation techniques for longer than I can stand to think about. Some people think teaching relaxation is all a sport psychologist does. But I can't even remember the last time I did anything remotely like that with a client. Why? Because, as I explained to Liz and her dad, there are so many better things to do—such as helping you to . . .

• **appreciate that maybe you're not supposed to be all that relaxed for a competitive event.** Shows do involve riding in front of a lot of people, with two or so minutes to do it right, with no "do-overs," with a judge watching. . . . Hello! I know being nervous doesn't feel good, but I've always found it easier to accept show nerves as part of the predictable show experience. A cop-out? No way. Know why? Pretty soon being nervous becomes like background "white noise": You don't hear it.

• **direct your attention to learning to ride well in spite of show nerves.** If being nervous makes you tight, try practicing staying loose in one critical part of your body (e. g., shoulders, elbows). Don't try to "relax" your whole body; that's too much . . . too hard . . . too unimportant. Save it for the spa. If being nervous makes you timid and tentative, make a point to keep reminding yourself to ride more aggressively ("Keep your leg on *yourself*!" I told one rider who rode too quietly whenever her nerves got the best of her).

• **make changes in how you manage your show day, or in how you think about winning and losing.** In Liz's case, problem-solving meant approaching her trainer and coming up with a better plan for showing. And letting "good" be good enough meant that she learned to measure her worth as a rider not by just her last class but by everything she's ever put into her riding.

The only riders I've known who were really "relaxed" while competing got there by accident—either thrown into a class at the last minute or riding under some other unforeseen circumstances that made their expectations, well, soft. But once something matters, everything changes—including your anxiety level. This isn't odd; it's human nature. And the less we fight it, the less it interferes with our riding.

The funny thing about show nerves is that they're a problem only if you think you shouldn't have them.

SHOWING: TOO MUCH PRESSURE!

Elegant girl trotting into the ring,
Gets a call back; does it over again.
Rides pretty well, receives moderate cheers,
Smiles to the winner—but behind the barn, tears.

Think this little ditty is about poor sportsmanship? Think again. It's about the experience of a teenager who would have been happy with her fourth-place ribbon were it not for her parents and trainers and assistant trainers, who could not (would not?) hide their disappointment at a less-than-blue-ribbon finish.

Oblivious to her plight, these adults wonder why the girl's riding becomes listless. They wonder why she begins to skip shows. They are bewildered— almost outraged—when she wants to try lacrosse in the fall.

Lacrosse! they bellow. *What does lacrosse have to do with your riding? Don't be silly. You just feel that way because you didn't have a very good show last weekend. This week will be different. I'm sure of it.*

Parents, teachers, I'm advocating for youngsters here because many of them don't have the skills or insight or self-confidence to let you know their distress—except in such drastic ways as quitting the sport, or withdrawing, or becoming depressed. Until they're a little older and better equipped emotionally to speak for themselves, they need *you* to monitor the pressure they're feeling and make needed adjustments to reduce it. And don't let my opening example lead you to think such things happen only at A-circuit shows. Pony Club, university riding programs, spring trials—they've all been invaded by the perils of Performance Pressure. It is an equal-opportunity destroyer.

If your kid comes up to you and says she (or he) isn't happy riding any more, please don't panic, don't look alarmed, don't get angry. I don't care how much money you've spent already, how talented your child/student is, or how many horses deep into it you are. Your child is entitled to find that she's changed in the way she feels about this complex and demanding sport. What's important is that she handle the change responsibly. That means resisting the urge to walk away from it all without exploring why she feels as she does, and coming up with ideas to repair the rip in her relationship with riding before deciding anything for good.

Unless some serious burnout is present—or unless the kid just wants to put some other activities in her life (hardly a strange request, really)—this problem usually can be resolved. Your young rider can't resolve it alone, however. She needs you to help the process along.

Start by truly, deeply listening to what your kid says when you ask what has happened to her affection for riding. Sit still and quietly, even when you hear things you don't like. Ask her to tell you more. Like it or not, you'll need to be open to seeing yourself as having been part of the problem. In some circles in this sport, the pressure—both spoken and unspoken, conscious and not—from loved ones and other important figures to do ever better is unrelenting. It's true, too, though, that in some cases the pressure comes from the youngster herself, driven by a need to be perfect, the best, the favorite. It can become a monster.

I know it's not easy to partner teens in this way. "I've tried to help her, but she just won't let me," lament parents and trainers. No wonder: She is a teenager, after all, stuck needing support from the very people in her life from whom she's urgently trying to gain independence. The trick is to rise above this impasse long enough to gain ground on the riding crisis.

I recently worked with a nervous kid in a showgrounds tack room on the evening before her equitation-championship class. The next morning, she graciously but quietly accepted my congratulations on her impressive second-place finish. Only when I spoke with her trainer later that day did I finally understand the reasons for her reserve: The trainer was visibly, and vocally, disappointed.

That's the kind of stuff I can't fix in a tack room. *I* need your help, too.

ADIOS TO AFFIRMATIONS

Dear Janet: My bathroom mirror is pasted with dozens of little yellow sticky notes assuring me that I'm a confident rider. I'm trying hard to believe it, but all I wind up doing is muttering, "Yeah? Says who?"

Morning, noon, and night I practice saying these canned phrases about feeling self-assured and confident, but it's not sinking in. In fact, the only thing I'm getting out of this affirmation business is the feeling that my bathroom mirror is mocking me. Should I keep on keepin' on or abandon ship?—Stephanie

Scuttle the boat and abandon with haste, Stephanie. Here are the reasons why I stay as far away as I can get from this (supposed) performance-enhancing technique—and why I recommend to all riders that they do the same.

• **First, any method that encourages you to paste over whatever you truly believe in favor of what you wish you believed is counterfeit.** It promotes self-deception and does nothing to improve your riding. You'll just end up wasting valuable mental energy on efforts to trick yourself, which is likely to be as successful as trying to throw yourself your own surprise party. It'll never work because the larger part of you always knows what's true.

• **Second, using affirmations to help yourself (falsely) feel more confident will leave you vulnerable to being blindsided when you least expect or need it.**

Consider Wendy's experience at her first dressage show: "All morning long—brushing my teeth; loading my horse; riding in the warm-up ring—I kept telling myself I was ready for this show and feeling great about doing it. Not until I started over to the arena and saw the *genuine* confidence in the expression of the rider before me did I realize *my* confidence was bogus—and begin to panic. All that 'confidence' evaporated in an instant, leaving me feeling like an idiot at the exact moment I entered the arena. Some technique."

More like a reality check just waiting to happen.

- **Third, relying on affirmations can be dangerous.** It's bad enough trying to fake how you feel; but even if you make a mess of things, your bruised ego will heal. Fake your abilities or readiness, though, and you're an accident just waiting to happen.

OK, NOW WHAT?

Here's something you can do instead, Stephanie, when you find yourself feeling less than a hundred percent.

Start by simply being honest with yourself about how confident is confident enough—for you. You don't need the confidence of a timber rider if you're not jumping timber. There's room for all kinds of riders in this sport: bold ones, timid ones, even "unconfident" ones.

Riders assume that being unconfident is a problem, but it may not be if they're continuing to make gains and staying out of trouble and doing all they want to be doing with their riding. Some people aren't confident about anything in their lives, but they still manage to love and work and play and enjoy. Certainly someone could manage to ride.

Once you have your honest answer, Stephanie, consider the following.

- **Understand your (less-than-perfect) confidence level as something that doesn't keep you from doing what you want to be doing.** Then put your attention on your riding—specifically, on how it changes when you're feeling less confident and how you can compensate for that.

Or . . .

- **Having decided that feeling more confident in your riding is important to you, figure out what's not working in your program and change it.** Maybe you're overfaced. Or overmounted. Or ill-prepared. Forget the speech-in-the-mirror stuff and get going with a different program or different horse or different trainer or different barn or different discipline.

Life's too short to force square pegs into round holes. Be a happy, safe square or change the pegboard.

PUTTING IT BEHIND YOU

The blighted show. The blemished lesson. It threatens to make mince-meat of your confidence, all the while you're trying to remind yourself that whatever happened (a crash, a splash, an unexpected dash) was really *no big deal.*

Happens to everybody, your friends and trainer say. Tomorrow's another day; you'll forget about it. . . .

Well, what if you can't?

Amanda writes in with an incident she had over the weekend. Describing herself as an experienced rider, she says:

I rode for years as a lesson kid, bought a horse, went through the green, novice, and amateur hunters. I recently made a switch to the jumpers, the B-circuit level—no really big jumps for us. But during my lesson last Saturday, things got ugly and then they got uglier . . . wound up with a refusal and came off. This isn't a bad thing—it happens—I realize that. But then it happened again. . . . By now I'm starting to have a lot of mental difficulty. So I got back on, jumped some more, but I was nervous and my horse was nervous. My trainer had us stop.

I'm leaving for vacation, and my horse will get schooled while I'm gone. What I need to know is how not to "fixate" on that lesson the next time I jump. How can I leave it behind as just a bad day and a bad lesson? I keep telling myself I'm just an amateur and these things happen. . . . I don't want to start a nasty spiral. . . .

Amanda, how about composing a ritual to help you mentally separate what happened in your riding on Saturday from what will happen the following Wednesday or Thursday or Sunday? Rituals—such as weddings, bar mitzvahs, *bon voyage* parties, even writing a letter you know will never be sent—help us celebrate new beginnings and/or say goodbye to old phases of our lives or to bad events. They are terrific interventions for people who are (or are worried they're going to become) stuck somewhere in their personal, work, or recreational lives.

How exactly do rituals work? Mainly in two ways: as markers of progress, and as a means to put some aspect of the past (e.g., Saturday's lesson) behind you by creating a sort of *wedge* between past and present. For example:

Nancy, who loved riding out on long hacks, had a frightening and discouraging runaway after her horse's martingale broke; she was haunted by the experience. So she used the power of ritual to bury—*literally*—the memory and its accompanying residue. She took a few days to select the right location and to compose a guest list (trainer, spouse, barn buddy), then held a funeral service for the event. She dug a hole and, with all the pomp and circumstance due it, *buried* that broken piece of martingale with all of its memories of the incident. Done, goodbye, walked away.

Now, for you, Amanda, we need to come up with a ritual (or two) so that Saturday's bad lesson stays Saturday's bad lesson—nothing more, nothing less. Here are some ideas:

1. You take the page for that bad Saturday out of your date book and scribble over it all the negative things you felt, thought, said, or did during the lesson. Then, and with great fanfare, you mail it off to the US Postal Service's Dead Letter Office—with no return address.

2. Change your computer screensaver to say *All new weeks start with Sunday.*

3. You buy a plain, solid-colored balloon and have it filled with helium. On it, you draw with markers a picture of the fall you had on Saturday. When you return to the barn post-vacation, you march right over to the spot where you took your tumble and, in perfect time with your release of the balloon, yell out, *So long, Saturday!*

Sound funny? That's partly the point. Beside making the act of "getting rid of" Saturday's problem concrete and palpable, rituals—especially if they're playful—do wonders to break up the tensions surrounding events people worry will remain stamped in the mind forever. Rituals stamp in a different reality: one that says *you can let it go.*

IT'S JUST A SHOW . . .

Here's a letter from a rider frustrated with her difficulty doing at horse shows what she does so well at home:

I have a bad problem with "show-ring nerves." I don't feel especially nervous or anxious, but I don't seem to be able to do the things I know I need to do. It's almost as if the thoughts don't travel all the way from my brain to my legs, hands, seat, or whatever—or if they do, they're too slow!

Sound familiar?

No matter how well people understand in theory that riding at home and riding in competition are two different things, they're still surprised when they can't somehow beat that difference. Rider after rider, figuring she's done lines and met fences like these a hundred times at home, tries hard—and harder—to *make* herself find the spots, get her horse's head down, relax her shoulders. . . .

If only it were a matter of simple physical execution! We'd just say, *Do your stuff, eyeballs! C'mon, Snickerlumps, hurry and get round!*—and they would.

But they don't. Certain things can't be forced, and these responses of body to mind are some of them. Yet everyone keeps talking as if they can be . . . by sheer force of will . . . by trying harder . . . by being more perfect . . . Aagghhh! It's enough to make you crazy (not to mention your horse). Add a horse show to the mix and you turn up the burners on all of this.

Why do our minds and bodies act as if they're speaking to each other in different languages? Because anxiety changes everything. Here are some of the more "popular" nervous reactions:

• **The "Lost in Space" syndrome**—that floaty, disconnected feeling, as if you're watching yourself from ten yards away. *Awful!*—unless you can learn to make it work for you. (Some riders use the feeling to launch themselves into "the Zone": to get into that head set where they feel unstoppable.) Best remedy? Develop an "anchor" symbol—some song or motto that sharply reorients you and keeps you plugged into what's going on. One client of mine sang herself songs by the rock group Little Feat to help her "keep her feet on the ground."

• **The Tin Man syndrome**—where your limbs and torso scream for the oil can. You don't have Dorothy to rescue you, so practice taking mini-moments (which is about all the time you'll have at the in-gate anyway) during which you *invite* your shoulders to melt a speck. A speck. As you'd invite a young horse to take the bit. For a moment. A speck. Don't try to hold the relaxation. It'll come; it'll go. That's all right. Try it again in a moment. Ask and see. Be curious and kind to your body, not commanding.

• **Sensory overload**—where you can't tell whom to listen to first: your trainer giving last-minute instructions, your mother reminding you to hang on tight, the vendor announcing that fries are up, the gate steward calling your number, or yourself. Ignore them all and go for the ocean of silence inside yourself. It's there—really. Listen for it the same way you listen for the ocean in those big pink conch shells. Use magic.

• **Mistake-o-phobia**—where doing nothing on your horse seems safer than doing what could turn out to be the wrong thing. This one's a tyrant. It strangles like ivy. Run away when you see it coming—and purposely make five (mini, non-riding-related) mistakes that day just to show the Phobe you're not scared.

No matter which of these (or other) horse-show plagues you suffer from, the stinkin' truth is that anxiety does change everything. Our bodies misbehave (not from malice, but from dismay), our brains ignore us, our tempers chafe and spit—and our horses conclude that there must be something to get nervous about because we're so darned *weird*. But if you can stop pretending that it should be any other way, you just might become one of those people who ride *better* because it's a show. Fires that melt the butter harden the egg.

FITTING IN WITH THE A-RATED SCENE

Dear Janet: I am a fifteen-year-old girl who has ridden all her life. I've taken lessons with different trainers, but mainly my mom helps me. She's been taking me to small shows for the past three years, but won't take me to any A-rated shows. She says that I'm ready, but because we don't have a big truck and trailer, we wouldn't "blend in." I think we'd be fine, but I'm now also worried about embarrassing myself. I know I can ride as well as anyone else at an A show. What do I do? —Lori

It's never much fun feeling as if you're on the outside looking in, whether it be at school, a party, or a horse show. Some of the A shows can be pretty fancy, and appear as if there are all sorts of "rules" for fitting in, none of which are ever spoken out loud. Kids and adults somehow pick up that there are certain kinds of saddle pads, britches, and shirt colors that are acceptable, and others that are not. Those who attend frequently know how to skillfully manage the busy schooling ring, secretary's stand, and crowded grounds. Those who show infrequently can get lost in the whirlwind. A-rated shows are also much more expensive.

But those things, as intimidating as they may be, shouldn't altogether prevent someone who's ready to compete at an A show from being there. Almost all of the things that anyone really needs—a well-conditioned horse and rider, sparkling clean equipment and attire, preparation—are related to hard work and a good attitude, not a thick wallet. Here are some points for you to go over with your mom to ease the transition from small to big and demonstrate your sensitivity to what I think may be some of her legitimate concerns.

• **Expenses.** The bigger A-rated shows are more costly to enter. Bring this matter up directly with your mom to find out how much it factors into her reluctance for you to show at the A shows. Discuss together a horse-show budget, and see how it can be adapted to fit in an occasional show that is more expensive. For example, maybe you could give up a few of the smaller shows and swap them for one special bigger show you'd like to attend. Or, consider helping out with extra chores around the barn or your home, or even picking up a few odd jobs (e.g., babysitting, grooming) to help cover expenses. See if there is another rider who'd like to go with you whose horse you could trailer for extra money.

• **Game plan.** Think about what it is you want to accomplish by going to A-rated shows. Do you want to test yourself and your horse against better company, or against more challenging courses and jumps? Do you want to see what those shows are like? Do you want just to be able to say you've been to some bigger shows? Are you looking to go once or twice or are you hoping to show regularly at that level? Talk about these things with your mom, too. It could help her to be more accommodating to your requests if she knows what you are hoping to get out of it and how you see it as improving your riding.

• **As for that truck and trailer issue,** don't give it too much thought. Sure, you might roll onto the show grounds behind a gleaming, super-sized van carrying horses that have traveled through more states than you memorized for your last history exam. But we all start in different places; please don't let that stop you. In this sport somebody always has a nicer van, saddle, tack trunk, or horse. It sets an easy trap for people to think they're not ready to step into the big ring because they don't have the right "stuff." The real right stuff is the stuff money can't buy.

REMEMBERING COURSES

Dear Janet: My fifteen-year-old daughter has been riding for four years and competing for the last two. Last summer she began to have trouble remembering her courses in the pony jumper classes. Neither her trainer nor her dad or I made any kind of big deal about it. We chalked it up to a fluke. But now Emily is having trouble again, and I can see her starting to get worried as the show season approaches for this spring. Knowing how a little thing like this can quickly become a big thing (especially for a teenager!), we are all trying to low-key her memory blocks. Do you have any suggestions for her dad and me, and for her trainer? —Diane

Diane, your instincts were right on the money as far as trying to keep the pressure off your daughter in an attempt to keep a memory lapse (which happens occasionally due to stress, fatigue, pressure, flukes) from becoming a Memory Problem. I suspect, however, that despite how you and your husband and Emily's trainer have been trying to low-key things, Emily's anxiety has run off in its own direction, creating not a Problem but, as is typical with adolescents, a CATASTROPHE. Let me try to help you all rein that monster back in.

The first thing Emily needs is to know that this is a solvable problem. She needs to remind herself that, for years, she successfully remembered where to go in a ring full of poles and jumps. That mental faculty is still intact. What's preventing it from functioning as smoothly as before is her worry that it has abandoned her. It hasn't. It's just used to working on automatic pilot, and doesn't know what to do when someone tries to muscle in on its job. Emily is trying too hard.

The task for Emily is not building a better memory bank but rebuilding her confidence for remembering courses. At home, her trainer should make up various exercises over obstacles in the ring (jumps, cavalletti, poles on the ground) that include multiple changes of direction. Gradually, the exercises become longer and more complex, resembling the courses she might expect at a show. If Emily gets lost, her trainer says, "No big deal, just start again from there." Advise them not to analyze why she forgot but rather just keep the lesson moving forward. Also tell Emily's trainer not to have Emily begin over if she flubs up midway; people can get too dependent on starting at The Beginning and never develop the ability to pick up in the middle and continue on. Practicing this from an arbitrary middle point gives riders confidence that if they do get lost on course they know how to regroup in the corners and carry on.

Next, have the trainer practice with Emily remembering two courses at once, as she will have to do for classes with a jumpoff. Make each course short for starters, the first one six or seven fences, for example, and the "jumpoff" four fences long. Gradually increase the number of fences for each round. Again, if Emily forgets where she's going, reassure her that no one's mad at her and that she'll soon find her groove.

One other tip for Emily is for her to make sure she studies the last part of a course as much as the first. Often, riders review the beginning over and over and give short shrift to the last few fences. Most important, don't let Emily's anxiety about forgetting courses stop her from going into that show ring. Let her know (and mean it) that if she gets lost, then the only thing it means is that she's still too nervous about forgetting to let her brain do its job of remembering. It will do that for her when she learns to trust it again. In the meantime, keep offering support and patience to your girl. This is one of those paradoxical riding problems that will go away when everyone stops worrying about when it will go away.

SOME LIMITATIONS OF VISUALIZATION TECHNIQUES

Dear Janet: I've been trying out some "visualization techniques" I read about in an article on sport psychology for riders. I was hoping that they could help my performance during my dressage tests, for which I invariably freeze up and make silly mistakes. But ever since I started trying to visualize perfect tests, I've begun to have even more problems. The more perfect my visualization, the more frustrated I get with my real (less-than-perfect!) ride. I guess I must not be doing it correctly, because it's really not working. Can you help me figure out what I'm doing wrong? —Samantha

Samantha, be relieved to know that there is nothing wrong with you and probably nothing wrong with how you are going about visualizing. The problem is in the fit between you and this particular sport psychology technique, and in the fit between the technique and this sport. Actually, I don't ever recommend visualization techniques to riders, for a number of reasons outlined below. Riders who have benefited from them shouldn't fix what ain't broke, but most people experience the same disappointment and frustration you describe, Samantha, and for them, as well as for yourself, there are other, more effective ways to improve your ability to perform under pressure. Following are a few reasons why some people struggle with visualization techniques:

• **First of all, any mental exercise that idealizes the notion of "perfect" is a deal-breaker in my book.** Being perfect belongs in romance novels and beauty contests; it has nothing to do with riding horses whose energies are far too dynamic to be bound up in such a term as perfect. Perfect is not a living term. Table settings are perfect. People and animals are not. People who try and make themselves perfect drive themselves (and those around them, including their horses) crazy.

• **Therefore, trying to recapture in real life the "perfect" visuali-**

zation you imagined the evening before is a perfect (ha!) set-up for frustration. You are chasing a dream. Inspiration is one thing, but to me, this dream is more like a tantalizing nightmare. Meanwhile, YOU ARE FORGETTING TO RIDE THE HORSE YOU HAVE UNDER YOU AT THAT MOMENT!

• **Want a great formula for non-spontaneous, non-free riding?** Tell yourself to replicate a previous ride. Any one will do—real or imagined. Do it exactly the same way. I mean exactly. Having a little trouble? Getting so wrapped up trying to copy yourself that you are distracted from your better, freer, more spontaneous riding ability? Of course. You can do this experiment without leaving your chair. Just write your signature down on a piece of paper, and then try and copy it exactly. I mean exactly. Cross the "t" in the same spot, dot the "i" with the same-shaped dot. Same loop in the "l"! Make your "p's" the same size! Same thickness! Oops! Which signature looks more natural? If each signature were an example of your riding, which would you prefer?

If performing causes you to freeze up in the ring, Samantha, rather than focusing on trying to ride more perfectly (too abstract a goal), consider trying to compensate for the ways in which the freeze affects your riding. Probably you wind up "under-riding": Unsure of your decisions, inactive and unclear in your aids, you "go along for the ride" and your horse makes up his own test. If you were to think instead about maintaining a more active stance, even if it meant you over-rode in your first few shows, I believe you gradually would be able to break out of the habit of freezing up.

Doing something different in your riding—even one thing—during those anxious moments can be the trick to triggering a different response to your performance nerves. For many riders, it beats dreaming.

STOP TAKING IT OUT
ON EVERYONE ELSE!

Dear Janet: When I go to horse shows, I tend to get very emotional and snap-
py toward whoever is around me, even when that person is helping (like my
boyfriend, who has come along with me to groom and help with my horse).
When I'm in the ring I'm fine, totally focused, but outside the ring I'm
screaming at my horse and/or boyfriend, blaming them for everything from
a smudge on my boots to the class before mine running late! Once I get out
of the class, no matter if I've done well or not, I am always more relaxed, and
then I feel terribly guilty about being mean. What can I do to keep myself
more relaxed before my classes, and consequently make life easier for my
horse, my boyfriend, and me? —Roz

R oz, there's a lot you can do to make life easier for all concerned but it
has nothing to do with getting yourself more relaxed before your classes. It has to do with holding yourself responsible for pulling the punch.

It's human nature to want to *feel* better before making yourself *act* better, but the truth is that it's an indulgence most relationships can't afford.
No one ever should have to wait for courteous treatment from a loved one
while that loved one tries to figure out how to feel less nervous or less angry
or less anxious or less depressed. You may not be able to help feeling lousy
from time to time but you sure can help taking it out on the people around
you. Our families, communities, and societies are stripped of civility the
moment we make accountability for our actions contingent upon how we
are feeling; otherwise, anyone can dismiss a tantrum, malice, or plain old
miserable company on having had—ahem—a bad day.

If you find yourself feeling nervous before your class, Roz, remember, so
do most. Feeling that way does not make you more entitled than anyone else
to lash out at the people who are trying to help. You must take steps to stop
yourself from indulging your temper. If you don't, you'll become only one

more nervous rider who has conveniently defined herself as a diva. Here are some ideas to steer you in a different, and more becoming, direction:

• **Learn to recognize the signs of your anxiety**—before everyone else does. You must become an expert at picking up on the first signs that you are becoming uncomfortable, agitated, impatient, or short-tempered. Consider if it comes to you as something you feel physiologically (i.e., butterflies, dry mouth, general physical tension), or as a way that you start thinking about things (i.e., thinking very negatively or catastrophically), or as a way you start acting (i.e., hurried, careless, forgetful). Don't get caught up blaming yourself for how you feel. You can't control that, and being nervous isn't the problem anyway. Besides, too many riders use that as a distraction from holding themselves accountable *for what they choose to do with how they are feeling.* People choose to let themselves lose their temper—or they hold themselves in check despite the impulse to cut loose. They choose to allow themselves to speak harshly, get sarcastic, or call someone a name—or they learn to assume that the other person is probably doing the best he or she can under difficult, stressful circumstances. They choose to say, "Oh, I couldn't help it, I was just really upset"—or they say, "I'm sorry, I let fly and I shouldn't have, and I'll make sure it doesn't happen again."

• **Select one or two strategies you can be prepared to put into effect** whenever you find yourself about to bubble over. They can include taking a two-minute private walk, repeating a personal motto, or simply telling your helpers that you are feeling nervous—an effective, honest way to defuse tension.

• **If you slip up and start cutting loose in a way you'll later regret,** don't figure, "Oh what the heck, I've already blown it, I'll just keep going…." Stop yourself, and explain to your boyfriend that you were doing the thing you used to do, but will stop.

• **And, finally, apologize.** For stubborn people like myself, the prospect of having to apologize is often a good enough prompt to do the right thing in the first place. Maybe, Roz, it can be for you, too.

LOST ON COURSE

Dear Janet: My mom and I both ride in jumper shows, and we both have a terrible problem of forgetting courses. I can forget where I'm going after only the third jump. My mom usually makes it through the first round but then forgets her jump off.

We do this all the time—not only in shows. We've tried writing the courses down and visualizing them, but neither helps much. It's really frustrating. Please help. —Fran

Fran, let's first check that you and your mom aren't making . . .

TWO COMMON MEMORIZATION ERRORS

1. Do you go over and over and over the first part of the course (or dressage test) and shortchange the last part? Many riders can easily recite fences 1 through 4 or 5 but are hazy about fences 7, 8, and 9—because every time they make a mental mistake while studying the course, they go back to the beginning to start over. By the time they reach the ring, they've been through that beginning countless times but barely touched the last third of the course. To be sure those later fences get equal time, I tell riders to study the last half of the course first sometimes, just so it doesn't get neglected!

2. Are you so focused on remembering everything in sequence that you have no way to recover and continue on if you momentarily forget your way? (You're in a similar fix to that of the child—and the many adults!—who can't recite the alphabet starting from some arbitrary point, such as K or N, but have to begin with A.) One good exercise: Practice memorizing the course from, say, fence 8 on; then from fence 5 on. Keep doing that until you become confident that you can remain oriented at any point on course, no matter what kind of bobble you have.

MORE TIPS

- **When you begin memorizing your course, chunk it down to bite-size sections of two to three jumps each;** study it in those clusters. Later you can string the clusters together to get your whole course down. This is easier than trying to memorize all ten or twelve jumps in a row right from the start.

- **Associate each jump with something else besides its number.** Let's say the final leg of a course is a bending line of three fences, all painted yellow and green; you could link their placement on course and their color with a rhyme: "Last line, lemon-lime." Worried you'll miss that right turn to the red planks? Associate the initial letters of direction and color; tell yourself, "Right to red." See someone sitting with a boxer dog at the far end of the ring? Say, "After the boxer, I go jump the oxer."

- **Don't settle for memorizing just from the bird's-eye view of the course drawing, or from one spot on the rail.** Learn the course using the perspectives you'll see it from while riding—from the ground and from different directions (away from the in-gate, toward the in-gate, et cetera). For example, mentally put yourself at the far end of the ring, turning back toward home. What will you see? How will the fences look from that direction? How will you know exactly where you're going? Many riders study the course from one part of the ring only, then find themselves disoriented by the view from the other side—by which time they're riding and looking the wrong way through the triple.

- **Give yourself lots of time to review your course.** Some of us (myself included) need more time than others to sit quietly and go over the course without worrying about having to hurry and get ready or get on. My personal experience has always been, "The more hurried I get, the more I forget." Time is more than a great healer; it's a super aid. Take it. It's free.

PERFORMANCE BLUES

The mailbag speaks:

" . . . My trainer says I sometimes allow my emotions to get in the way of my riding, but I'm not sure how to handle it. It's as though I feel someone will beat me if I make a mistake, and I can no longer relax and enjoy riding because of it. . . ."

" . . . Soon I'll begin to compete. . . . I'm nervous and don't know how I'll handle the pressure. . . . I'm afraid I'll mess up in some way, and in the process will lose. . . ."

" . . . would like to bring up a topic I have trouble with—not being good enough. My parents spent all this money, and I feel that it's all going to waste because I'm not a good rider. . . . I don't want to just ride for fun. I really want to be something!"

I plucked these letters from among the bunches because they so perfectly reflect what's involved in an issue I have written about recently: performance pressure, when what you've been enjoying suddenly becomes a burden. There are two ways to respond: You can try to hone your ability to ride well under competitive conditions, or you can try to relax the standards of riding to which you hold yourself when competing. Most people work strenuously to do the first and wind up with problems from trying too hard. Few consider the second, which, paradoxically, usually buys you the first.

What would I tell these guys if they came into my office? Something like this:

• **Finding the solution to pressure may require some backpedaling.** Where and when did things change for you? What was different then? Did your goals change? Or your trainer's? Maybe your spouse's? Did you buy a new horse, or switch barns or instructors, and then find that everything had changed? Can you go back to the old way? Would you *want* to, if you could? Or would you rather find a better way to be where you are now?

- **Make managing competition nerves** *part of your riding program.* (I'll come back to this in a later column.) Don't separate this piece out, making it something to get rid of, or to conquer, in the week before your first show. Mental skills are simply part of the plan—like developing a deeper seat, a more educated hand, or a better eye.

- **And this business about emotions getting in our way—who's kidding whom?** Of *course* they get in our way! We're not robots. *Learning to use our emotions in constructive ways* is a lifelong challenge, hammered out in the riding ring, in the boardroom, in the bedroom, at the Thanksgiving dinner table.

- **You already** *are* **something.** Period.

- **This pressure, where's it coming from anyway?** From you, with your own well-defined hopes and goals? Or from someone else—a spouse, parent, trainer? Sometimes it's hard to tell—one starts to feel like the other, and then you can't pick out where it's coming from any more. . . . If the pressure is of your own making, then why has it become so important for you to win? One client of mine, in for depression, told me that whenever she lost a tennis game, she used to feel as if she, as a person, was a loser. Once she learned to separate her day-to-day accomplishments from her sense of self-esteem, she became less frantic about succeeding in or winning everything she was involved in. She also became less depressed. And if the pressure is coming from someone else—well, you'll need to speak up.

- **Afraid of messing up?** Everyone hates it. Everyone does it. Give yourself a wider margin for error or you'll shrink your world down to something over which you feel you have total control. Sadly, it will be a very small and lonely world.

- **And, finally, remember:** Try for a grander perspective on it all. You're not judged on any one class or show. The picture you create as a rider is bigger than that, which makes everything easier. There are many, many ways to demonstrate your riding, and to show your *self* through your riding. It's all in how you present yourself, and how you present your horse, how you treat him, how you speak about your wins and losses, the grace with which you handle a wrong lead, a refusal, a spook, an elimination, a bad lesson, a bad show. A *winning* rider is not always the one with the blue ribbon.

YOURS, MINE, OR OURS?

You're at a horse show. You're standing around waiting for your class to be called, pulling at your ratcatcher, and thinking that you'd rather be back at the barn, hacking in chaps and shorts. You're also so nervous that you can hardly see straight, and the egg-and-bacon sandwich you bought from the food truck is doing a rumba in your stomach.

Suddenly you have an epiphany—you know, one of those rare moments in your life in which you discover and understand the essence of something. And what you understand is that being at this show and doing well are really not that important to you. They're important to someone else. Well, now what? The "problem" with insight, always, is that it drops you off at the doorstep of having to take action. In this case, that action is speaking to the people whose wishes, inadvertently or not, you've been following.

For many this is the stumper. "Speak to him/her/them? What would I say?!" Well, there are any number of things you could say, but maybe the following will help you get started.

To your trainer: "I know you get excited for me to do well at shows, and I appreciate your confidence in my riding. But, to be honest with you, this year the pressure to win is getting to be too much. I'd like to slow it down a bit—maybe not show as much, maybe do more out on the trails. I know you're really into showing, but it's just not as important to me as I thought it would be."

To your husband or wife: "I really love having someone who cares enough about my riding to be this involved. But, to tell you the truth, sometimes I feel as though I have to win in order for you to be happy. I start thinking I'd better do well to justify spending all this time and money on riding! Would your feelings change if I worked less on winning and more on just enjoying my horse again?"

To your parents: "I want you to know that I feel very lucky to have you, because you've been really good to me in terms of my riding. But sometimes I feel pressure to do well, especially if we've just gotten a new horse, and especially if he's expensive. I feel bad if I don't win on him, and I don't want to feel that way because I'm not having as much fun riding as I used to. Plus, I'm getting very nervous now at shows. I need to know it's OK if I just do the best I can."

But don't let it all end there. Ask the other person for his or her thoughts. Get a response. Make sure you at least have *some* feedback, so you know where things stand. For example, some trainers may *not* be as interested in working with you if your goals change significantly. There's nothing wrong with that; everyone is entitled to occupational preferences. Those preferences just need to be out in the open, so you then have the option to change to a different barn where the climate and/or values are different.

If you have questions, ask them. Invite your trainer/spouse/parents to ask you *their* questions. Keep the conversation collaborative, not adversarial, and say what you need to in order to make your riding work for you. If there's tension, ask what the *two of you* still need to do to get rid of it.

And there's more, because things aren't always that simple. In some cases riders mistakenly experience their own feelings and desires as having come from others. Why? Some of us are uncomfortable with our own competitive or perfectionist strivings; instead of accepting them, we attribute them to other people: "I don't care about winning! *He* does!—the old "pointing fingers" technique. Called "projection" in psychologese, this dandy little mental gymnastic allows us to own up to only those feelings and thoughts we find acceptable. The rest we give away.

How do you discover what *yours* is? The way anybody does: You learn to listen to yourself, whether you like what you hear or not. And after you've allowed your own message to come through, then you decide what changes you need to make in order to live your truth. It's much easier to go along for the ride—be it show nerves or something else—when you know the ride is of your own choosing.

RATTLED BY NERVES

Dear Janet: I am a capable rider with a willing and experienced horse. I show in the appropriate division for our skills (3-foot jumpers), and have a lot of confidence in my trainer, who prepares us well for the few shows a year that I enter.

My problem is that I don't show a lot, so I still get really nervous and distracted every time. What happens then is that I wind up riding below my ability. Small things tip me off my game, for example, another horse stopping at a fence, even one that my horse jumped fine while schooling. The other thing that happens is that all the jumps look bigger and spookier than they "really" are. Even seeing the videographer or hearing a friend's encouraging comment can make me lose my focus! Then, if I make a mistake on course, I start wondering how bad I must look to the audience rather than putting my attentions on what's coming up next.

I could be winning and not just getting by on this horse. So how can I learn to make my show rounds more like any other jumper round?

—Shellie

Shellie, you can't make your show rounds more like any other jumper rounds because they're not like them. They take place at a horse show, where there are judges and videographers and people standing by the rail watching you. It's different. You're different. Sometimes your horse will be different. Jumps do look bigger and spookier and I can't tell you exactly why. It's a perception thing. But what I *can* tell you is that the more you try to treat the two situations as the same, the more you will feel their differences. And that's a human-nature thing.

Your expectations of yourself are too high, Shellie. There are gobs of riders who have been showing for ages still getting nervous before and during their classes. Some will get better with time and mileage; others will learn not so much to "control" their nerves as much as learn to compensate for how their anxiety affects their riding. If it turns their legs into a vise, they learn to think in terms of riding more softly. If it turns them into silly putty, they learn to think in terms of riding more decisively and assertively—not in terms of more "relaxed." If, like you, the anxiety makes them orient to every possible distraction in the environment, they learn to remain generally focused on the matter at hand while hearing this or noticing that.

The belief, Shellie, that focus has to be impenetrable undermines the confidence of many who would otherwise be able to attend to several things at once—their course, their ride, their trainer's last-minute instructions, their name being called out over the loudspeaker. Fluidity and flexibility is the name of the game here, not shutting out. Shutting something out is forced. Not orienting to extraneous stimuli is something different, never forced, and a talent of the most mentally adept athletes: think of a World Cup rider headed into a trappy triple, Nadia Comaneci on the vault, Muhammad Ali's eyes.

Shellie, rather than trying so hard to duplicate at shows the performance you are able to deliver at home, put your attentions on riding as well as you can that day, under that day's conditions, with the distractions that present themselves then. Recently, a wise horseman helping me with a green horse said that if I were able to recover, while jumping, 20 percent of that horse's suppleness and roundness from the flat, then I should be satisfied. That was good enough. Let the level of riding you are able to recover on show day be *good enough* for now, and take pleasure in watching the gap between what you can do under ideal conditions, and what you do when nervous, close over time.

PERSPECTIVE

I just finished Joan Ryan's *Little Girls in Pretty Boxes*, an astonishing book about the destructive training system used on our elite female gymnasts and figure skaters. The book describes the tragic courses many of these girls' lives take as a result of greed and desperation run amok. The physical and psychological costs are startling, as are the rationalizations coaches and parents and sports officials offer for their allegiance to this cruel program designed single-mindedly to make Olympic medalists.

Our equestrian Olympic contenders are not the vulnerable and impressionable fifteen-year-olds of gymnasiums and skating rinks, and so are spared the ruthlessness of some coaches. Granted, the stresses on riders are enormous, even by adult standards, but they don't result in the severe eating disorders, multiple stress fractures, stunted bone growth, and psychological humiliation that happen to these young kids. But all of us, Olympians or not, are familiar enough with competition, even if it's only with ourselves, to identify with the experience of these little gymnasts and skaters—girls who, in their fervent desire to win, to be recognized, to be the best, find themselves having lost their bearings and sacrificed too much.

Pressure, writes Ryan, is like a virus that affects each person differently. For some it energizes, emboldens; for others, it becomes an enemy to be beaten back. I would add that for a lot of people it's both, that sometimes the edges between the two blur, and that at times they seem so alike it's hard to tell the difference.

How can you tell if the pressures of wanting to do better, or be the best, or simply be the best you can be, have begun to take over the show (pun notwithstanding)? For me, the bottom line is always whether or not these pressures take away from your enjoyment of this sport. But there are other signs that you've been derailed by your desires to win. Take a look:

- **Mood changes, such as chronic irritability, especially around the** barn; people telling you to "chill," or that you've become "too intense"; increasing conflict with family members, barn-mates, or trainer about riding

• **Riding when advised not to**—by your doctor, for instance—or riding in spite of physical pain or your better judgment

• **Using your horse against your veterinarian's or trainer's recommendation**

• **Spending more time or money than you should on advancing** (most of us do this anyway, but I mean *really* more than you should)

• **Finding yourself getting angry with your friends or barn-mates for winning more than you,** or for having better horses, more money, more time, et cetera

• **Getting so competitive with your trainer that you've stopped yourself from learning from her or him;** e.g., not letting her school your horse for you because you "can do it better anyway." (If this is true, then you should be considering a more advanced trainer.)

• **Increasing frustration with losses at competitions,** especially frustration that's out of scale with the situation

• **Feeling a compelling need to "do well" or win** in order to justify keeping or showing your horse

• **Experiencing doubts** about whether or not it's all "worth it."

One swallow does not a summer make, so don't become too worried if this list includes a few things you've felt at times. It's when these things become regular visitors in your life, and begin to affect your relationship with your sport, or with your friends and loved ones, that you need to reflect on how you handle competition and what meaning it has for you. Riding, I've come to recognize, offers occasional opportunities to learn more about ourselves. Sometimes it's more than we want to learn, or more than we feel we want to do anything about. Fair enough—not everyone is on a path to psychological enlightenment. But seeing ourselves against the backdrop of competition can tell us a lot about those things we value in ourselves, and where they stand in relation to other things that we *think* we hold dear.

[CHAPTER 2]

Confidence Building
Recovering from Falls
and Managing Fears

WHAT'S GOING ON HERE?

Of the scores of letters I've received in response to my column, the overwhelming majority deal with fear and riding. People are frightened of getting hurt, of becoming disabled, of being laid up with family to care for. Writers include kids and adults, novices and seasoned, those who ride for pleasure and those who show. No community of riders seems immune.

Some of you who've written have already experienced horrible riding accidents. Others of you have had smaller-scale mishaps leaving a taste of just how bad a bigger mishap could be; you become like survivors of minor earthquakes, living in fear of the big one. And some of you have never had anything happen, but your fantasies of misadventure wreak more mental damage than most real calamities ever could. Yet hardly a letter closes without expressing your devotion to the sport, love of horses, and commitment to overcoming the bugaboo of being afraid. How is it that we can want something this badly that scares us so?

Several weeks ago, my husband, John, was organizing his breeches and tie and jacket the night before a show. A novice rider, he was preparing to enter his first 2'6" division since years ago when, overmounted and terribly overfaced, he fell off five or six times in nearly as many shows. His goal for this year was to successfully complete, on a trusty school horse, two jumping rounds in a manner that didn't terrorize (or embarrass) him.

John was nervous and knew it. I asked him if he thought he was going to enjoy his show. He replied that he wasn't enjoying it yet, and probably would not while it was happening, but that tomorrow at the end of the day he probably *will have* enjoyed it immensely.

John's not alone in his "push-pull" feeling toward riding, and his retroactive gratification. Daily and in droves, riders far more white-knuckled than he walk, pedal, and drive out to their barns despite their trepidation. Some of you tell me of virtually forcing yourselves to get on. This is not the anxiety of performing that sport psychologists always talk about—this is being afraid of getting hurt. When you finish your ride, there is no athlete's high, no euphoria; the feeling is one of relief. You are happy to have simply returned to the ground on your terms, and on your feet. And then, marveling at the complexity of your relationship with this sport, you do it all again the next day. Simultaneously loving and fearing riding, doing and avoiding it, you remain devoted.

But why are so many of you riding scared in the first place? Should there be this many? Granted, riding has significant built-in risks, but you have to wonder if something within the industry is unnecessarily aggravating riders' fears.

Some worries are a natural consequence of such life events as getting older, having children, shifting priorities. Many of you write of returning to the sport after years away, having not only a different (and less resilient) body to deal with but a different psychology: "I used to gallop around and never worry about getting hurt! What happened?" Other worries are an unfortunate consequence of those accidents I mentioned earlier.

Most of these fears are treatable—but, better yet, can they be prevented? Are our training, instructing, or horse selection/purchase methods inadvertently creating riders who are not comfortable on the backs of their own horses? And if so, what needs changing, and who—trainer, rider, parent—is in the best position to spearhead such a movement? I think we've all seen too many bad green horse/green rider combinations; people write that they can't afford anything but the greenie. We've seen people ride in divisions or lessons that they're not prepared for; people tell me they only have time to ride twice a week. Everyone is trying to do more with less; it only mirrors the rest of our busy lives.

Maybe there's a better way. The idea of looking for such a possibility reminds me of a parable I first heard in graduate school: A man walks over to a crowd gathered by the riverside. He sees villagers frantically pulling people out of the water one by one, hour after hour. It finally occurs to the man to travel a bit upstream and see who is pushing all those people in to begin with.

DON'T 'JUST DO IT!'

Everyone loves a slogan—especially one that gets us over the hump of inertia or fear or self-doubt. But cheering yourself on can backfire if the cheer is premature or misguided.

WHEN SLOGANS DON'T WORK

I see this happening to many riders who, spooked by a bigger fence, greener horse, or trappier cross-country course, use slogans to try to charge through their trepidations—often with disastrous results. Sure, anyone can need a push of encouragement now and then when trying something new. But this column refers specifically to situations in which, against their better judgment, riders mount up on horses that are too much for them or attempt to do things that are over their heads.

These riders worry about "giving in" to their fear, disappointing a trainer, falling behind in a training schedule. They ride on because they "don't want to be a baby," or because someone told them to. Some, like Julie, do it because they think it's the right thing to do.

Hello, Janet. I have developed a fear of jumping. I've never been an aggressive rider, but now I get so tense approaching a jump that I hunch forward and freeze mentally. I have a good instructor and have started using a horse that is very dependable, but I wonder what else I can do.

I used to jump three feet, but then I stopped jumping for two years because of no time and no trainer. And while this horse is generally a good guy, sometimes he leaves a stride out and I end up on the ground. Should I keep jumping small fences until I'm comfortable? Or should I "just do it" and get over it? —Julie

In a word, Julie, no. Don't "just do it." Not only will you not get over your problem; you probably won't get over your first jump. Slogans are great inspiration only when they suit the situation. Overfacing yourself mentally in this way sounds dangerous to me.

SKILL-BUILDING, NOT SLOGANS

Instead, do the following:

- **Go back to your other idea, jumping small fences until you're comfortable.** Not only is it safer; it's the truest, fastest way to dissolve your fear of jumping. It will let you gradually become and feel more competent, secure, and psychologically comfortable with the task at hand. That means you'll ride better, and *that* means your horse will go better for you. When the rides are consistently better, the fear gets replaced by a sense of mastery and confidence. The answer to loss-of-confidence issues in activities where there is physical risk is (almost) always to bring the person back to within her or his comfort zone and work up again from there.

This is different from the way I recommend dealing with mental fears, such as fear of making mistakes or of not being able to control everything. There I encourage people to act in spite of their fears, because nobody can ever be "perfect" enough or have that much control. Relief from those fears comes only from doing.

- **You need to have more control over when your horse is leaving the ground,** which means doing exercises that develop your eye for distances, his adjustability, and your judgment about how to ride lines of fences with related distances. You'll then have fewer "surprise" takeoffs—and fewer undesignated landings.

- **You can also help yourself with your fear by doing things that make you feel more secure in the saddle.** Ask your trainer for exercises to strengthen your lower leg and seat and improve your upper-body balance. Longe-line lessons, frequent use of low gymnastics, riding in two-point are all good. Also, leave your stirrups in the tack room every once in a while and walk and trot, walk and trot.

USE THE FEAR, LOSE THE FEAR

Don't get into a screaming match with your fear, Julie, or try to muscle it away. You could wind up feeling more afraid or getting hurt. Instead, treat your fear as a clue that something in your program is amiss—a fire bell of sorts. It's not about being tough; it's about being smart.

SHOULDN'T I BE OVER THIS BY NOW?

Dear Janet: Recently I had a bad experience that I can't stop thinking about. I asked my horse for a canter on a loose rein to warm him up. . . . I had spurs on . . . lost my stirrup. I got him with my spur, and he picked up speed until we were in a full, out-of-control gallop . . . finally bucked me off! Broken bones, weeks of bed rest. . . .

It's been two weeks since I started riding again. The first time was great. And then my horse tripped and I went flying off . . . no damage, just a good scare. Now I'm terrified . . . try to pretend nothing is wrong, visualize myself riding safely, but it's not working. Instead of concentrating on my serpentines, I'm wondering how far the hospital is from the barn. . . . Need help! —Liz

One of many similar letters, Liz's request for help following a frightening riding mishap speaks for hundreds of her equestrian companions — as do her efforts to overcome her fear. Unfortunately, these methods usually only make the problem worse. Let me explain.

Liz, I admire your positive attitude and your efforts to get back mentally to where you were before the original fall. But something very scary did happen to you. And it's through no fault of your own that you still feel frightened riding, worrying that at any moment your horse may run off again. That's how people who've had something bad happen to them react. They're always feeling that the "bad thing" could happen again, that they must be on the lookout all the time. It doesn't make for a relaxing ride.

Ironically, getting over this kind of fear involves accepting it and understanding why it can't be wished away. First, it serves an evolutionary purpose: Eons ago, those cavemen who respected their fears survived the best. Of course, the dangers were a little different (rock avalanches, mountain lions), but our bodies are still pretty much wired the same way. Second, we have vivid memories; we *remember* the panic of the runaway, the pain of our injuries, the frustration of being laid up. And finally, as creatures with fore-brains, we humans attach meaning to incidents and put them in a larger con-text. A fall isn't just a fall but a month out of work, a month without income, a month with no one to muck or feed or tend to the rest of the family.

Pretending that something didn't happen or didn't affect you doesn't work; the larger part of you always knows what's true and what's not. And visualizing yourself riding safely, Liz, won't do a thing until you really *feel* safe riding again. A visualization can't overpower a worry (and shouldn't, in case it's a "good" worry). I prefer you use visualization to enhance or enliven a feeling you *already have*.

So, what can you do? I recommend what I'd tell anyone who suffered a trauma—*and you did suffer one*: You take a deep breath, pat yourself on the shoulder for trying to get back in the game, and become as supportive and patient with your own self as you describe your trainer and friends being with you. You start slowly, you take your time, you stick to gaits and exercises you're comfortable doing, and you build from there.

In your case, Liz, the sequence of steps might be: With your trainer or a knowledgeable friend present as long as you need her, ride comfortably at the walk; ride on a loose rein at the walk; trot comfortably; trot circles at each end of the ring without worry; trot a serpentine of just two loops; then trot on a loose rein, trot a three-loop serpentine, and so on. Wait until you *want* to take each next step; when you feel ready and eager, take it and see if it's OK. If you become nervous, back up; try again another time. Your trainer or friend can help you decide when to try, and can provide the encouragement you may need to get over the hump. How long should each step take? As long as it takes. Learn to value your moving toward goals as you value your attain-ing them.

This is the most dependable and safe way to get back to where you were; it allows you to heal *naturally*—always the preferred way. If you were a pro-fessional who needed to get back in the game fast, or a World Cup contender with upcoming grands prix you absolutely had to ride in, I'd suggest other strategies. But for you, for now, riding within your comfort zone will allow you to enjoy your horse while watching yourself return—gradually, *securely*—to your former self.

CHALLENGED OR OVERFACED?

Dear Janet: A few weeks ago I started leasing a new horse. He's pretty advanced, and he gets really hyper when we start doing canter work or jumping. I ride him alone sometimes, and he can get out of control. When I canter, he bucks; if I make him trot, he goes very fast or tries to break into a canter again. He's hard to control—and simply pulling on the reins doesn't help. I don't think he's being bad, just excited. What can I do to get him to slow down and put his mind on his work? —Mary

The appeal of a bigger, stronger, more powerful horse over a docile and trustworthy one is hard-wired in many riders' minds, and nowhere is the tale more eloquently told than in Walter Farley's *Little Black, A Pony*. A lovely children's book, written in 1961 and sketched in all the burnt oranges and olive greens of that era, it tells the story of a young boy whose desire to see if he could handle the "can-do" horse on the farm, Big Red, led him to temporarily abandon Little Black, his beloved and trusted companion of many years. This universal theme sounds in Mary's letter.

But a match made in heaven this one isn't, Mary. What you are calling "advanced," I would call either too green or too fresh or too bullish. The only thing advanced about this horse is the level of rider needed to handle him.

If you were to keep this lease—which, from the information you've given, I wouldn't recommend—there are several things you'd need to do right away. The first: Get a good trainer to help you learn to manage this horse better and to keep the situation as safe as possible for you and the horse. Out-of-control horses get themselves and their riders hurt; that's the main reason why I don't like this choice of horse for you. Another reason: Even if you make it through the lease unscathed, you won't learn a fraction of what you could on a horse whose manners and schooling allowed you to focus on your riding rather than on staying on board. Moreover, in many cases, riders on horses that they cannot control stop enjoying riding.

As you've discovered, getting this horse to slow down will involve much more than pulling on the reins. Developing your other riding aids and learning how to use them effectively will help. So will professional guidance about proper equipment (appropriate bitting and saddle fit), barn management (is the horse getting enough turnout? getting too much feed?), and constructive exercises on the flat (nix the jumping until you have better control) that will enable you to get his attention and respect.

The hardest part of all of this, Mary, may be your feeling disillusioned. In some cases people lease in order to have a taste of the kind of horse they couldn't afford to buy, then are disappointed to find they can't ride the darn thing. In others, riders are just looking for a less expensive way to ride on a regular basis and lease whatever horse is available in the barn, whether he really suits them or not. Thinking of the lease as a "for the time being" arrangement, they overlook features they wouldn't accept were they buying. This can be a mistake; bad habits, fears, and accidents can develop or happen quickly. The "wrong" lease is never short enough.

Can you find another horse to lease, Mary—one that's quieter and better mannered? You don't need fancy, and you don't need top-of-the-line schooled. Old could be good; plain could be lovely. Forget "advanced" and look for safe and sensible—the kind that gets passed over precisely because he's old and plain. You'll learn, you'll have fun, and you'll be protecting your love of the sport by averting problems of lost confidence.

Farley's boy strayed only a short while before returning to his furry little pal—pride, by itself, can ring hollow after a while. The boy found that all the admiring glances he got while tooling around on the big sleek bay could not hold a candle to the deep pleasure and companionship he got from Little Black. He also learned there were some things his pony could do that the red horse couldn't. Smart boy. Dear, invaluable story. Maybe that's why it remains my favorite kids' book.

LET HISTORY REPEAT

You fell off your horse while out riding and now are afraid to ride in open spaces. . . . Your horse ran away with you on your first hunt, and now you're terrified to ask him for a canter. . . . Your horse and you did a "crash and burn" through an oxer at your last lesson, and now you shiver at the thought of jumping anything that has more than one set of standards attached to it. I could go on and on with examples plucked right out of your letters, and the sheer volume of them is testimony to how pervasive an issue fear is. Let's tackle the issue again, this time with an action-oriented twist, one that can help you overcome your fears by using a resource you already have: your own history.

For many of you, the limitations that fear places on your riding are only one part of a miserable experience. Another is the sense of despair that can creep in when you try to get out from under your feelings, only to find you can't *will* them away. So then you try some visualization or thought stopping. And when that doesn't work, you feel not only hopeless or resourceless, but inadequate or even depressed as well.

But the situation is not hopeless, and you're not without resources. You have them in the shape of memories and experiences that hold different pieces of the answer. You need to weave these pieces into a tapestry of know-how and support and inspiration that can move you through your predicament.

Were you ever afraid of learning to drive? Did you have difficulty as a kid going on sleepovers? Were you nervous about going off to college? Have you ever been scared to board a plane? Give a talk? Ride a roller coaster? Ask for a raise? Relocate? Go back to school? Well, what did you do to push yourself on? Did you learn more about the area to buttress your confidence? Did you get somebody to help you? Did you practice extra hard, more than you would have ever really wanted to? Did you temporarily scale down your goals? Did you take a gradual, step-by-step approach? Did you take a self-motivating course? Did you talk with a therapist? Did you learn to surrender to the absence of control (i.e., on the roller coaster) and simply enjoy the experience? Did you wait and start anew a few months later? How have you been able to surmount other situations when you were afraid to do something? *These are your problem-solving abilities.* Your task now is simply to direct them at a new target: your fear of doing something around or on top of a horse. Psychological skills are skills, whether you use them at home, at the airport, at work, in the amusement park, or in the riding ring.

If you got over your fear of returning to school as an older student by gradually increasing your course load over time, apply this same step-by-step approach to your fear of jumping, for instance, by learning to jump one new kind of fence every two months, or by increasing the height of the fences very gradually. If you got over your fear of flying by reading about the mechanics of flight, then read books about working around horses on the ground to get over your fear of leading, turning out, and longeing. If you finally gained the confidence to ask for a raise by consulting with an accomplished colleague who taught you how to step up and talk the talk, commit to contacting that trainer you've always liked and taking a few lessons organized around helping you with your fear of cantering. Make a game plan based on the problem-solving skills that have worked for you before.

There's one other terrific resource: memories of riding when you were *not* scared. Maybe the memories are far away and hard to recall, but most of you were, at one time or another, riding confidently, boldly, enthusiastically. Draw those experiences up again mentally, not only through your mind's eye, but through your recollections of this other time's smells, sounds, and body sensations. Refamiliarize yourself with this more comfortable, confident you in order to begin bumping yourself out of the rigid identity of "fearful rider." What was different then? How were *you* different then? What did you say and do and believe that allowed you to ride that way? How much of those elements can you bring into your life and your self again, now?

Dorothy found the answer in her own Kansas backyard. You can, too.

'IRRATIONAL' FEARS

Dear Janet: I am a sixteen-year-old girl with a very, very large fear problem that has no basis in fact. I am afraid to jump more than two feet. I have a sweet, willing, quiet gelding with a wonderful jump and an "I'll do anything" attitude. But if we get over a two-foot-six jump, it is considered a huge thing.

I love my trainer and I love my barn. I am not afraid of falling, getting bucked off, having my horse bolt, etc. I seriously do not know what I am afraid of. I have read countless books and articles, talked to hordes of people on the subject, tried so many visualization techniques, but nothing seems to work. I jump small and build up, but it hits a certain point and I panic. I am really, really afraid of ruining my horse. Please help. . . .

—Monica

I would love to, Monica. But, first of all, what is the push to jump higher than two feet anyway? It's a respectable if not massive height, and no manual I ever saw says you or anyone else has to jump one bit higher to be considered a bona fide rider. There is still a lot of fun you can have on your horse with what you can already do, especially since you are comfortable.

Perhaps, though, your barn buds are moving on to rated shows. I suppose that they're jumping higher fences, and that some of the pressure you feel to do likewise comes from not wanting to feel left behind the pack—no picnic, that, I know. But in pushing to stay with them, you risk losing what you currently have: a happy rider, a happy horse.

I'm not convinced the bigger fences have your name on them right now anyway. To my ear, you sound comfortable when the fences are two feet high and uneasy when they are higher. Why push it?

But if you do have designs on the bigger divisions, or a quest to get to a higher level of riding/jumping, then there are some things you can try. One is to build up to a bigger jump more slowly. Two feet three inches sounds nice, for example—especially at the end of a welcoming line of low fences with related distances. You could just do that one exercise with your trainer for as long as you need to feel right about the new height. Another is to learn to jump higher fences on a lesson horse—so you get most of your own kinks out before asking your fellow to step up.

Remember, too, that you don't have to do it all this year. Maybe next October you'll casually look over to your trainer and say, "Hey, I'm feeling pretty good today. . . . Why don't you put 'em up a hole?" There's no better medicine in this sport than time.

Worried about ruining your horse? Only if you talk yourself into biting off more than you can chew. If that happens, your apprehension will become his. Let somebody else teach him how to get his behind over three feet, or two-six. Or you teach him later, when you've mastered the height. Or don't teach him at all. He doesn't care. He really doesn't.

And most important, don't think of yourself as having fears that are "irrational," as if there's something wrong with you. Many would say that the people jumping big fences are the irrational ones, and that you make sense.

Monica, your not understanding your fear doesn't mean the fear is irrational. It could mean that you're clever at masking the source of your discomfort at two-six. For all we know, what could be happening is that you're good at two feet and don't like feeling (or looking) not-so-good, the way you might for a while with the fences raised. It could be that a part of you knows that if you did become accomplished at two-six, you'd feel a strong urge to do more showing, which would precipitate some tension at home. Or maybe two-six is simply too high.

Could be this, could be that. Doesn't matter—understandable reasons, all. Irrational? No, just un-obvious.

That's OK, though. We don't need to know everything about why we do what we do in order to enjoy our horses. We only need to respect the messages our bodies/minds send up.

Relax a bit, enjoy your sweetie, jump your two-footers for now, and try it all again when you hear that extra six inches calling your name. It'll wait for you.

THE SPY WHO STAYED HOME

A woman came into my office and told me she had become frightened of riding her green horses. Kathy hadn't fallen, and she hadn't been run away with. She was just more and more uncomfortable doing what she'd done for years. She vaguely mentioned getting older and said something about being very independent. She lived alone.

I asked what would happen were she to get hurt on one of her young charges. "I really don't know," she replied. "I don't have anyone to help me out. I have a few friends who would do what they could, but no one to, you know . . . "

"Yes, I know," I said. "No one to drive you back from the doctor's office, to make your breakfast the next day, to clean out your cats' water bowls, to turn out and feed the rascal that dumped you. No one like that." She softly agreed.

Kathy, it turned out, never really had a "fear" problem. She wasn't afraid of getting hurt. She was afraid of getting hurt *and then having to realize the limitations of the independent lifestyle she'd enjoyed for years.* Without realizing it, Kathy had grown afraid of a truth about herself—one that was hidden behind a fear of riding green horses.

Kathy isn't the first rider whose worries masqueraded as a fear of riding. I once worked with a little boy who developed a "fear" of jumping at Pony Club; it turned out to be his way of putting the brakes on a hobby that was causing tension between his parents about money. A woman whose marriage is stressed by the demands of competing away from home might feel conflict about perfecting her upper-level movements because a part of her knows that as soon as those movements are polished, she'll be hitting the road big-time—leading to more stress.

Now what am I supposed to do? you wonder. *I'm having a hard enough time getting over these little jumps; I need to start worrying about what it all means?!*

Can't I just be scared without it meaning anything else?

You bet. Simple, unadulterated fears are the ones that resolve with patience, changes in your program, confidence-building exercises, and the like. They respond to sensible measures.

But fears like Kathy's are different. They *don't* respond to such measures. They linger, get worse, cause secondary problems (e.g., you start arguing with your trainer, you stop wanting to take lessons). They could be what's going on if your efforts to deal with your fears aren't working.

So what do you do? Looking for the fear behind a fear may sound challenging, but figuring stuff out about yourself can be made—well, if not exactly fun, at least interesting. Here's how:

Think of your fear—the "symptom," we'll call it—as a communiqué in a secret code from a hidden part of yourself that's trying to send up a message. Your job is to break the code and figure out what the message is.

Now, you may not like the message. That's why it's sent up in code—because that hidden part isn't sure you're ready to hear what it has to say (e.g., *I'm afraid to move on because I'll have to leave my beloved pony for a fancier horse*, or, *If I do this course well now, everyone will expect me to do it perfectly from now on*, and so on). The message may not even be valid (no one is really expecting you to do a course perfectly forever more). Nonetheless, you need to be open to new messages, trusting that you'll be able either to correct the mis-assumptions or to respond to them in more constructive ways than becoming afraid.

Another way to glimpse the secrets you keep from yourself (we all keep secrets from ourselves) is to consider—as honestly as you can—in what ways this symptom would actually be *helpful* to you (e.g., give you a good excuse for leaving your trainer, getting a new horse, avoiding arguments with a spouse). Fears work very hard sometimes to make things happen in ways we will never suspect. And all for no thanks.

These fears are stubborn but not meaningless. They cry to be heard, but no one's been paying attention. So they dig in their heels and demand that you listen. Can you hear them? Will you?

'BUT I REALLY AM AFRAID'

A young girl of thirteen writes in that she's become afraid of riding her twelve-year-old Quarter Horse. A little high-strung, the horse gets quick with her and doesn't respond to her aids. She tries telling her trainer about being scared she'll be run off with or fall, but the trainer says only that she worries too much. "Nothing is going to happen to you," he tells her. She wonders how she can convince him that she really *is* scared—and, more important, get him to take her fears seriously.

This scenario between rider and trainer is very common. And trainers aren't the only ones who may not take a rider's fears seriously—riders do this to themselves all the time. They dismiss their fears as childish nuisances, mask the fears with overconfidence, or chide themselves for feeling as they do. These are terrible things to do to oneself, and they usually don't help the situation anyway.

As far as I'm concerned, a rider's fear is *real*—it's not a debatable issue. What it feels like to her (or him) is what it is. Period. It doesn't matter whether her trainer, barn buddy, college professor, mother, or grandpa thinks she is overreacting, overprotective, or overindulgent.

Besides, once a rider feels a situation to be dangerous, it has usually become at least mildly so, if for no other reason than the negative way her uncertainty affects her riding. And forget altogether about trying to talk yourself or your student out of the fear—logic has little currency in the playing fields of emotion and anxiety. So the immediate objective between trainer and rider becomes that of limiting the rider, for the time being, to a zone of riding in which she feels comfortable and safe. (Yes, there are times when a rider needs her trainer to encourage and even push her forward. And there are a number of things she can do within herself to overcome her fears. Both, however, are topics for another column.)

Let me get back to this young girl with some recommendations for how she might proceed at this point:

- **Approach your trainer when neither of you is riding,** and tell him you need to talk more about feeling scared when riding your horse. Talking while unmounted gives you more time to explain how you feel than you'd have during a lesson. Also, during lessons, it's too easy for your trainer to say, "Oh, go on now, just try it and you'll see you'll be fine. . . . " If your trainer isn't free at that moment, set a time later that day or the next. It doesn't have to be a big deal; just ten or fifteen minutes will do.

- **When you do sit down with your trainer,** take your time explaining that you really are becoming more and more scared to ride your horse, and that you've tried to make yourself believe that "nothing will happen," but it just isn't working. Ask if he has some ideas for making your horse less high-strung (more turnout, less grain, getting him schooled more, different tack) or for making you feel more comfortable on him (riding under your trainer's supervision only, riding on a longe line, more work on basics, lowering the fences, using a smaller ring). Try to keep the conversation going until the two of you come up with at least two ideas you'll feel comfortable trying.

- **Consider involving your folks in this process as well.** Let them know you've been feeling unsure about your horse. Maybe they can be helpful in convincing your trainer that a different approach to your fear may work better. Perhaps, too, they can join you in your talk with him.

People are always very surprised at how much their anxiety lightens when they feel they're being heard and taken seriously by those who matter to them. There's another thing that being heard does, too: It moves the people who hear to share responsibility for monitoring the anxiety level— so, for example, our rider (especially since she's a young rider) doesn't feel she has to track it all by herself. That's a hefty load for most, and too much at thirteen.

PANIC ATTACK!!

Dear Janet: I have two gorgeous horses that now do little more than eat grass, get groomed, sleep, and poop. They used to have jobs—that is, until an "incident" occurred. The incident involved one of the horses bolting with me during a lesson, and then taking off at a full gallop around an open field. Too stunned and scared to do anything, I sat there frozen like a Popsicle stick. Finally I "came to" and managed to stop him with a hearty pulley rein.

I thought I was fine until I went to ride my other horse the next day. No sooner had I put my foot in the stirrup than I was overwhelmed with the most awful feeling I'd ever had: I was sure I was having a heart attack and going to die. I put my horse away and went home, thinking I'd try again the next day. But when I did, the feeling was even worse, and it's been building ever since. Now I start getting panicky as I'm pulling into the barn driveway. I feel like such a baby and am getting very frustrated. I've been riding for twenty years and should not be afraid to get on my horse—especially the one that didn't run off! How can I get over this stupid nonsense and get on with my riding life? —Sheila

Sheila, you've joined millions who develop panic attacks at some point in their lives, usually after an out-of-control, frightening incident such as the one you described. Be assured, though, that the attacks usually do diminish and eventually resolve with time and with thoughtful management of the predicament at hand.

Here are a couple of things to keep in mind:

• **You're not a baby.** Your panic attacks are not stupid. They're trying to remind you that something scary happened so that you can prevent it from happening again.

• **Don't try to ignore or strong-arm the panic.** Getting blind-sided by panic when you least expect it while riding (e.g., as you're about to cross the road on a countryside hack) or ground-handling horses (e.g., as you're about to pull your horse off the trailer or handle a breeding cover) is potentially dangerous. Accept your panic as part of your current experience—as much as you may resent it—and deal with it matter-of-factly. Here's how:

• **Take time to consider what part of the incident was most anxiety-provoking.** "What part? The whole darn thing!" you say. But wait, Sheila—was it the loss of control, fear of injury, feeling embarrassed, horse falling in a groundhog hole? If you can isolate the worst aspect, then the problem won't diffuse into a general avoidance of all things having to do with riding.

• **Consider what changes you are willing to make in your program for the time being in order to render it more comfortable for you to ride.** Staying out of open fields? Riding only with supervision? Refraining from cantering/jumping/riding alone? One rider I knew was too proud not to canter; she rode at Second Level. But she experienced panic attacks after a bad fall at the canter, and rather than slow things down for a while until her confidence was built up again, she refused to ride at any level less. She's still refusing, and it's one year later. Saving face by insisting on doing everything you've always done even though it is making you a nervous wreck is short-sighted. Regroup, take it slow, ride smart.

• **Forget about trying to make the anxiety disappear.** Focus instead on making the feelings manageable, tolerable. Remember that you don't have to like how you are feeling in order to ride. Doing this will help lower your need for everything to be back to normal immediately. Eventually, the anxiety should become less intense or occur less frequently. If it doesn't, consult with professionals about the appropriateness of your training program or riding level or choice of mounts. Most riders who have become comfortable with the level of risk they are assuming in their equestrian activities have programs and horses that suit them well.

• **Finally, select one or two reorienting phrases to help you in times of impending panic or during the attacks themselves.** Something like, "This is not a heart attack, it is a panic attack," or, "This will go away, I won't die from this," may sound silly in the light of day but can be just the ticket when you feel your heart about to burst through your windbreaker!

STRETCH YOUR COMFORT ZONE?

Dear Janet: I've been riding for as long as I can remember and have always been a little cautious around horses. Recently I got a new lesson horse to ride. He's a big horse with tons of muscle, and he's also somewhat pushy. A while ago he became lame and couldn't be ridden for three weeks. When I started riding him again, he was fresh (of course) and played all kinds of tricks on me. I wanted to ride him through all his shenanigans, but I just couldn't do it. My trainer told me that I could have ridden him through it all; she's also always telling me that I don't like to go outside of my comfort zone and that I need to push myself a little more (bigger jumps, etc.). I also feel I need to push myself more at times, but I don't seem to let myself do it. Can you help?

—Esther

Wow, everybody's pushing here, Esther! Your new lesson horse, your trainer, and now you, too. That can work if it's what you want—but many riders I know find themselves being pushed along far faster and harder than they ever bargained for and end up unhappy. Below are some points to consider in figuring out how to progress and keep enjoying the horses at the same time.

JUST BECAUSE YOU CAN DOESN'T MEAN YOU HAVE TO!

Whether you can or can't ride through it is irrelevant. A better question is *do you want to?* Having the mechanical skills to do something isn't enough reason to forge ahead if you don't have the mental readiness or desire. We all can probably do lots of things, but we choose what we prefer to (or have to) do. Should it be so different with our riding? Remember, it's not your job. It's your sport or hobby. Make it work for you.

WHAT'S SO BAD ABOUT BEING "COMFORTABLE?"

A lot of riders spend day after day challenged by work and family. Pushing the envelope is the last thing they want to do when they drive up to the barn. I would be saying different things to an aggressive, competitive, going-places contender, but not everyone has designs on competing at Rolex or Gladstone. Unless you have some riding goals whose achievement matters more than comfort, ask yourself what's so bad about staying in your comfort zone in the first place. Many riders *like* their comfort zone. They don't want to leave. They only do it because they've convinced themselves or someone has told them that they should. They may have been told it's the only way to progress. Leave the "no pain, no gain" stuff to the Marines and explore other lesson programs that advance students gradually.

YES, SUCH PROGRAMS EXIST!

I hear it already: "Janet, sounds good, but where are the programs that let me learn at my own pace?" They're around. I don't know of a systematic way to find them yet, but try researching it on the Internet. Or look in your area for barns or schools whose staffs are sensitive to differing learning styles and have a focus on customer satisfaction. I've casually run across a couple of such programs—and I'm not the only one finding them, because they all seem to have one thing in common—long waiting lists!

One more point before I wrap up, Esther—this one about the other side of the "comfort zone" border . . .

IF YOU NEED A PUSH, GET A GOOD ONE

You mention being cautious by nature, so maybe you *do* need a nudge to keep yourself moving along. Just make sure you get a good push: one that's directed solely in your service and your horse's. (If those two services conflict, change your mount.) Good pushes take into account your riding strengths and weaknesses, are graduated, and build confidence. They help you disassemble your apprehensions bit by bit and don't characterize them as irrational or stupid. A good push also respects your wishes—and can be put on hold at any point where you change your mind. Some days you feel you can and some days you feel you can't. Some days you just don't want to. Your prerogative.

BUZZ LIGHTYEAR'S LAMENT

The letter begins:

"My wife is fifty and I am fifty-three. . . . We are concerned about injury and want to preserve our ability to ride well into old age. Can you tell us what issues face us older riders? There is always the concern that injury will not only interrupt our riding but cause more permanent disabilities. Christopher Reeve's injury has made us all think. . . . " —Ray

This letter from Ray represents yet another twist on the theme of fear and riding. It deals with age and aging, with bodies that might break instead of bend, with the chills felt when someone gets hurt. It deals with how we change over time, physically and mentally, and the adaptations we want or are forced to make in response to a process beyond our control. Here are some issues older riders face that younger ones don't:

1. The final erosion of adolescent invincibility, which never really ended at nineteen—you know, that part of us that said we could do anything, anytime, anywhere, and nothing bad would ever happen to us. It's a little like what Buzz Lightyear went through in *Toy Story* when he learned that he really wasn't an all-powerful space ranger but just a toy, vulnerable to breakage, obsolescence, abandonment. Older riders may not become obsolete or be abandoned, but they can break—and may find that what might have been a sprain years ago is a fracture today.

2. Higher stakes in terms of injury. A younger rider misses a day or two of school or work. Older riders tend to have more responsibilities: tuitions and/or mortgages to pay; retirement to save for; established careers with obligations that aren't easily postponed. Especially with fewer earning years ahead, lost income and lack of independence and mobility can have distressing consequences.

3. The developmental passages to be navigated as you get older—such as menopause, becoming a grandparent, turning fifty—*and the meaning they have for you.* Of themselves, these events need not make people more worried about riding—but they can. One client of mine associated her impending menopause—because of the condition's connection to osteoporosis—with a sense of physical fragility. She *didn't have* osteoporosis, and she *wasn't* fragile, but that was the meaning she'd subconsciously given this phase of life. Becoming a grandparent made my mom feel alive all over again, but someone else may see herself getting "really old."

How do you counter these thoughts?

• **Keep fit, and focus on your health and the aspects of yourself that are young and vibrant and robust.** Try to avoid long breaks from riding, so that "getting back to it" never becomes an issue. If you must be away, do what the pros do: Work out on the road, or at home if you simply can't get to the barn. And if you feel at all insecure when you start back, ride with a trainer or knowledgeable friend until you're secure in the saddle again.

• **Maintain an athlete's frame of mind.** Take your riding seriously—and have a few witty retorts on hand for when you're asked if you haven't ridden "enough" by now.

• **Accommodate your changing abilities, mental and physical.** Actively map out new programs with new goals that are suitable for you now but *just as appealing* as your old ones. *Different doesn't have to mean less!* Explore other equestrian activities, even other disciplines.

• **Redefine your feelings of being fearful as being *more careful*.** You're not chicken—you're using good judgment!

And re: Christopher Reeve . . . well, there *is* risk. However, you can stack the deck a lot in favor of safety by never overfacing yourselves, by picking your mounts wisely, by working with a trainer for new or riskier exercises and for comebacks, and by investing in good, safe equipment. Then select a level of play that balances your safety needs (which may not match someone else's) with your pleasure and athletic needs.

Remember, too, Ray, what else your letter said: *"We love what this sport has done for us as a couple and for us physically. We always had plenty to share, but now riding has become our obsession. What fun we're having!"*

OF COURSE YOU'RE FRIGHTENED

Dear Janet: I have been riding since I was four years old. I am now forty-four and have recently taken up dressage after several years of not riding at all. All of a sudden I'm afraid! What is wrong with me? I was never like this when I was younger. My new dressage horse is a warmblood, and very sensitive. If I am working him very hard and he becomes tense, his head will come up, his back will hollow out, and he will scoot out from under me for a few strides. It's very scary. My trainer and I have worked very hard at keeping him relaxed; I also had his teeth done and had him checked for physical problems. Every time I get on him to ride, I am terrified—my hands sweat and I feel fear. What's causing this and when will it go away? I've been trying to talk positive talk to myself but my mind just keeps saying, "You can't trick me with those phony words!" What can I do? Thanks! —Chicken Little

Repeat after me: "There is nothing wrong with me. And my name is not Chicken Little." Let's start by giving you a new name. I like Lila. So let me help you, Lila, reorient to your unfortunate (but hardly surprising) situation, point by point:

• **Why be so surprised to find yourself afraid after a several-year hiatus?** Several years off in your thirties and forties is different than several years off in your teens or twenties, in the same way that a nine-year age difference in a couple is a bigger deal when they're twenty and twenty-nine than when they are forty and forty-nine. The matter is not insurmountable, but does require extra attention.

• **That horse you bought** . . . sounds a lot like the horse you *expected* to be able to ride upon your return to the sport. I'm not sure it's the horse you need to be riding right now. Oh, how I hate to rain on a parade, Lila—but—a "sensitive" horse for an anxious, just-started-riding-again rider? I don't know. You will not be able to *make* yourself relax enough to keep him from becoming jiggy, hollow, or scooty. And you shouldn't have to. As an amateur rider, you should have your needs served by your horse, not the other way around. Incidentally, hard work, *if correct,* will not make a horse go worse. Can you get another opinion on how well you and your horse work together?

• **That "positive self-talk" stuff?** Lose it. Quickly. Of course your mind is saying you can't trick it with those words. It's like trying to give yourself a surprise party—the larger part of you always knows what's true and what's not. You insult yourself when you try and fool yourself into believing something you already know not to be true.

WHAT TO DO INSTEAD

• **Put away the calendar and get off the clock!** Give yourself half a chance to get beyond the anxiety by allowing for however much time you need to regain your confidence and security in the saddle (psychologically, not just physically). There are no shortcuts here. But here's the dilemma: the only way for you to become more confident and secure is to have repeated confidence-building experiences, which you are not getting on your new horse right now.

• **So, can you change the way you are riding him for the time being?** Consider trying, for instance, an easier program that doesn't get him tense. If it would make you feel better, why not just walk and trot for a while? You wonder how long is a while. Until you are so comfortable and confident and bored on his back that you feel hungry for something more. Think of your sweaty hands and your fearfulness not as your enemies to be manhandled but as valuable cues that you are overfacing yourself. Stop what you are doing then, and change something. Riding in that condition only courts trouble.

• **Keep a perspective on all this,** Lila, that allows you to see your return to riding as a process and not an event. Don't rush it or you'll risk your love of riding. The fears you disdain are legitimized by virtue of their presence and strength; that's enough "why" for now. The important thing is that you respect your trepidation and alter whatever you're doing that makes the problem worse. The way out, Lila, is through the middle, nice and slow, step by step.

NOT AFRAID ENOUGH

Dear Janet: I have the opposite problem from the one your readers usually write in about. They usually are concerned because of how afraid they are of their horse, or of cantering or jumping. My best friend at my barn isn't afraid of anything about riding, and sometimes I think she should be. She's very brave, and rides very well, but sometimes I think she takes too many chances with her and her horse's safety. We're both event riders, and she thinks that being a good event rider means you never back off no matter what. Sometimes she's just too aggressive and overfaces her horse. He goes only because he's more afraid of her than the fences. But I worry they are an accident waiting to happen. She's single, very independent, and as stubborn as they come. I love her dearly. Anything I can do? —Jenn's Best Friend

You are a good best friend, JBF, but you are rowing upstream. A rider as bold and capable and competitive and stubborn as you described isn't much interested in toning things down, especially for the benefit of friends. Nonetheless, there's still a conversation you can have with Jenn, at least to introduce other perspectives that could take shape later when—with maturation—her judgment begins to supersede her bravery.

Let me start with a little commentary. There are many different reasons why people will seem to be so darn brave about stuff. Lots of times it's because they are genuinely so darn brave about stuff. They've been brave since they left the hospital where they were born. They crawled into places that would scare most other babies, stared curiously when others would have cried, squealed with pleasure when their fellow toddlers would have turned and run away shaking. They rode the most dizzying rides at the county fair, and jumped into the deep end before they knew how to swim. They scared their parents long before they ever scared you and me.

There are other people though who, to the casual observer, look to be as brave as the day is long. In earnest, they are quite anxious about the challenges they have assumed. But maybe they think that having trepidation or doubts means that they're weak, or that people will think they'll never accomplish their dreams. So they hide it from others, sometimes from themselves. They ride horses, jump fences, and work at gaits they aren't sure they should be trying. They call themselves terrible names to try and make themselves buck up and accept the challenge. They get hurt. They quit.

Jenn sounds like someone from the first camp—inherently bold, a going-places kind of woman. She's going, whether anyone goes with her or not. Unfortunately, she may end up going alone, if she overfaces her horse and loses him in the process. But maybe that's where you can enter the picture. Tell her how much you admire her dauntless nature, her derring-do. Tell her that sometimes you think she's so brave that she carries both herself and her horse, and sometimes you worry that, as confident as she is, her horse might suddenly realize that he's acting braver than he really is, and get scared. Tell Jenn what you told me—that you love her dearly, don't want her to get hurt, and are willing to risk her being upset with you because you can't keep your thoughts to yourself anymore. Then tell her that you won't bring it up again unless she asks you to.

Were Jenn a minor, or under your training, or boarding in your barn, you would have a stronger platform for expressing your concerns. But you are "just" a friend, albeit a dear one, and Jenn is lucky to have you. And the truth is she is a big girl, and doesn't appear to be looking for input. If things get to a point where you can't even stand to watch Jenn ride anymore, don't, and be sure to tell her why you can't. But stop short of telling her that she should do something about it if you've already spoken your mind. Saying something more frequently that the other party wants to hear it will not make it sink in any better; the reluctant listener is more likely to turn off altogether. Sometimes the best thing a good friend can do is to make it easy for the other person to come back and say that you were right after all.

AM I READY TO MOVE UP?

Dear Janet: I'm an amateur hunter rider in my early forties who has appreciated your articles about how to safely and patiently deal with fears and recover from bad riding experiences. Could you write something about how to determine when it's safe to push yourself a little, and face some of the anxiety. I've spent the last year bringing my confidence back from some bad riding experiences (falls, dealing with a stopper), and now have a new horse that's a gem. He's fourteen, done it all, and clocks around whatever course is in front of him. I haven't shown at 3 feet for two years, and want to again very much, but am not sure if I'm ready and how I'll know when I'm ready. We school fine at home, and have been showing in the 2-foot-6 and 2-foot-9 divisions. I feel ready to move up, but I'm worried I'll get nervous at the shows and go back to bad habits (riding defensively) or miss all my fences (I don't have a great eye and it gets worse at the shows). My trainer generally isn't one to push but says it's time to get going. What do you think? —Leslie

Here's what I think: Of course you're going to get nervous. Of course you will be visited by some of your old habits. Of course you are going to miss a few distances. It can't be any other way in the beginning. But none of those is necessarily a reason not to move forward.

Leslie, if your horse were green, with little tolerance for mistakes, or if you felt that missing a distance meant a crash and burn, then I'd say, "Wait, the stakes are too high, and the margin for error too low." But your worries seem to be related to a fear of making embarrassing mistakes, rather than a fear of making dangerous mistakes. This is a good thing; we can all survive embarrassment better than we can physical trauma. A rider who strongly fears the "bad" things that could happen were she to press on is telling herself and her trainer that she's not ready. A rider who fears humiliation at the out-gate is ready to be shepherded into the ring.

Below I've listed three considerations for taking some of the guesswork out of the equation of whether or not to move up. In the end, it's always a matter of judgment, but it never hurts to try to stack the deck in favor of it being the right choice.

• **How well can you trust your assessment of this situation at this time?** Even the most level-headed rider in the world can get overeager with a new horse and a renewed dream. You, Leslie, sound like you're in good shape to tackle the next division: Your horse is seasoned and reliable, you're successfully schooling at home what you would be doing at the shows, and you seem mentally ready. People who have a tendency to be reckless or impulsive need to be very careful at these times, while those who by nature are overcautious may need a nudge from their support team. You seem pretty balanced.

• **Contrast your prospective gains and losses.** Gains look good for you, Leslie: a return to a prior (higher) level of riding, the accompanying feeling of triumph, fun times with your new horse (who does sound like a gem—I wish more riders in your situation would consider these trusty veterans for partners). Risks? Not so bad—intermittent hiccups of an old habit until you acclimate, a missed distance or two. All manageable. The habits will diminish significantly as you accumulate positive experiences and learn to ride less defensively; that's a time-and-mileage thing. And the misses? Forget about them—everybody's eye gets worse at shows because we're all nervous and trying too hard to get it just right. As long as you can get to the other side of the fence safely no matter how badly you miss, Leslie, you'll be fine. And so will your horse. That's a packer's job.

• **Are there junctures in your show day where you could bow out gracefully should you change your mind about doing the 3-foot classes?** Feeling stuck with your "commitment" will only make you more anxious about the whole thing. Knowing that you could decide you don't like the courses or don't like how your horse schooled and want to drop down a division is a liberating thought. It's also good horsemanship.

Moving up while scared of getting hurt is never a good idea. Moving up while nervous about how well you'll pull off the challenge is part of the territory for a competition rider. Resilient mounts and supportive trainers make it an even safer proposition. Yours seems a favorable situation for moving up, Leslie. Review the points above with your trainer and let her help you choose the when and where. Be nervous, make mistakes, get better, have fun!

[CHAPTER 3]

The Psychological Side of Riding, Learning, and Training

A DIFFERENT KIND OF
DEFENSIVE RIDING

I saw a young man ride today
With quiet on his face.
I looked more closely, watched him move,
And saw a different place
From which he lived and
breathed and rode—
It wasn't calm at all.
It was the stare of 'I won't care,'
Of 'I won't let this matter.'
I try to skirt the things that hurt—
Like disappointment's batter.'
I've seen this face a lot before
On those who say they can't endure
Their own berating private chatter
That feigned indifference is hired to shatter,
Leaving them to ride around
Void of heart, of light, of sound.

—J.S.E.

Several years ago, a professional rider in his early twenties visited me at my office. He'd sought a consultation because he felt dissatisfied with his career so far. In spite of the fact that he had good horses and good owners, he was having trouble maintaining his enthusiasm, especially for horse shows. To his surprise, he was feeling bored.

I asked how long he'd felt that way, and he surprised himself again by acknowledging it had been two years.

"I used to get so excited when I did well and when my horses went well. It was the best feeling. But then I started to feel as if every round had to be the best, and that if it were anything but the best, my clients and students would be disappointed and start to think, 'What am I doing with this *kid*?' At some point, the pressure to prove myself week after week got to me. I think I just decided that I wouldn't let it matter to me any more, that I'd grow a skin so thick nothing would touch me. And now nothing does—even the good stuff."

Some people ride defensively as a way to protect themselves from getting bucked off or having a nasty stop. And some ride defensively as a way to protect themselves from disappointment or frustration or embarrassment. Instead of sitting incorrectly, or maintaining a choking hold, they blame others for their mistakes, avoid new challenges, or act indifferent.

I told this young professional about a talented junior rider I'd known, a girl so afraid to let herself want something she couldn't *guarantee* she'd get (a great round, a win on a horse she'd worked hard and long with) that she convinced herself she didn't care. She spent her horse-show days shrugging off her losses *and* her wins, and eventually left the sport.

"Don't let yourself stop wanting what you *do* want, even though you're not sure you can get it," I told Michael. "Once you commit to a life of avoiding disappointment and loss, everything will just start feeling like flat soda. So will you."

Michael understood this. He resurrected his hunger to be the best rider and trainer that he could be. He graciously went forward into a sport and a career that alternately leaves its adherents elated and devastated—easily within the same day. Most riders wouldn't trade it for all the tea in China. Good for them. The kind of defensive riding Michael ultimately rejected usurps the best part of a rider: the soul.

LIVING WITH HORSES & RISK

Dear Janet: My green horse is coming along beautifully; with professional help, I am tailoring his activities to his physical and mental ability. But I have a growing fear of his hurting himself because of something I ask him to do.

We live in an area where foxhunting abounds, and I'd be thrilled to go. But if he were to step in a hole or catch a leg on a coop, I would feel devastated—because I put him in that situation. How can I enjoy progressing in the sport when I am so concerned about the possibility of injury to my horse? I willingly accept the risk for myself, and I would like to be more comfortable with the risks of injury to my horse so I can enjoy these activities that are available. Maybe I should just stick to my mountain bike. —Cora

Cora, your mountain-bike solution may be tempting (you're kidding, I know), but it would forever hold you hostage to a need for control that would shrink your world in the most awful way. You seem sensible and prudent, and your horse would probably love to go out foxhunting as much as you would. Stretch yourself, assume the risk, and live your life.

Might your horse step in a hole? Yes. Catch his leg? Yes. It wouldn't help you for me to say "probably not." There's no respite for the worrier as long as a fraction of a chance exists that the bad thing could happen. And don't bother trying to eject the "negative" thought from your mind; it's really not the demon everyone thinks it is. The bigger demon is the illusion that you can live a rich and gratifying life without learning to tolerate the anxiety that stems from the (human) limits of our control.

Decide what you really want to be doing with your horse and how emotionally costly holding yourself back would be. Understand that sheltering him from life won't make him a happier horse, either. Obviously, the more you do with him, the greater the chances are for him to get hurt. However, we all know that horses manage to get hurt doing nothing (so it seems), so "no activity" is no guarantee he won't. If you want to chase foxes and you have a horse temperamentally and physically suited to it, then go chase foxes and leave fate to whatever you believe handles it—chance, natural law, God. You cannot know what is going to happen.

Nonetheless, once you've decided to "go for it," stack the deck in your favor by getting the two of you properly prepped. That could mean more conditioning, more training for your horse, more lessons for you. Investigate to find out which of your local hunts is most suitable for you to go out with—hunts vary in terms of difficulty of terrain, fence height, pace, and mercifulness to newbies. Consider how you will know if you've overfaced yourself or your horse while out cross-country and how you'll be able to exit the situation. (If you can't—or can't at least drop the level at which you are working—you'll be in a spot that's unproductive and possibly dangerous. That's not the hunt for you.) Also, start with smaller events that simulate hunting: low-key paper chases, cross-country hacks with friends who'll be patient with your horse's need for gradual exposure, and the like.

Finally, Cora, understand that bad things can happen no matter how well prepared or careful you are. And if they do, it does not mean you are a bad person or irresponsible owner. You must find a way to be at peace with this or you'll forever be looking over your shoulder—waiting, wondering, trying to control events that may never occur. You'll be riding, but you'll be miserable.

Not long ago, I spent the first week after my new horse's arrival worrying endlessly about all the things that could happen to him. I tapered his old feed as I gradually introduced his new and still worried about colic. I clipped and dressed him, then added a layer of blankets, then took two off, then added them again and still worried about his getting too warm or too cold. I went on and on until I realized that I wasn't enjoying my new horse. So I told myself, "Janet, you are careful enough. If something happens, it happens, and that's the horse business."

And something happened. My brand-new horse fractured his hind coffin bone, all by himself, in a "safe" paddock. That's the horse business, I guess. Small and big consolation, both.

MIRROR MIRROR ON THE WALL

Dear Janet: I have been riding horses for over fifteen years and I've taken lessons with lots of different instructors on different types of horses—hunters, jumpers, event horses, dressage, some western, too. I now have two horses of my own and the problem is that my trainer doesn't seem to appreciate how much experience I've already had. She wants me to take lessons more regularly, and do lots of basic kinds of exercises on the flat with my horses. I feel very capable of training my horses on my own, with just occasional input. Also, her lessons are starting to bore me, as she has me jumping over much lower fences than I usually practice over. Do trainers always think their students need more and more, or do you think it is just this trainer? I'm worried she's holding me back. —Sherri

Probably no other sport indulges more our capacities for grandiosity than does riding. It doesn't matter how old a person is, or how long they've been riding. People who have been riding for six months will march up to a rental barn on vacation and ask for the "friskiest" horse available. Others, whose talent remains, uhm, unapparent despite decades of instruction think nothing of declaring themselves experts by virtue only of all their hours in the saddle. Scary.

This is balanced, of course, by the sport's equally matchless ability to humble its constituency within two shakes of a lamb's tail. Be it by introspection (rare), trainer feedback (more common), horse feedback (more common still), or competition results and videocam (most common), the majority of riders who stick with it long enough learn they have some gaps and holes, blind spots and delusions. None of this means that you are headed back to the beginner's ring, Sherri, but I would encourage you to be less offended by your trainer's input than curious, and see it as an opportunity to cross-check your own impressions about your progress with those of another. Kind of like balancing your bank account with your statements.

The real students of this sport know how the learning never ends and jump on every opportunity to learn more. Few would consider working without at least a groundperson, and many train all their lives. My father still wonders why I keep taking lessons; it's only been twenty-five years. "Haven't you learned how to ride yet?" he asks me. And all of the riders who have managed to climb their way to the top of the sport still go back to the basics, time and time again, throughout their entire careers. They understand that they have to, that good riding is premised upon a correct foundation, that it's easy to find retrospectively that you've physically or mentally strayed. The "basics" which you resent, Sherri, serve as your compass, and they are what bring you back home again.

That said, let me suggest to you some specific points to think over. It might help you decide how you want to proceed.

Consider what it is you want to do with your horses and why. Many riders prefer the quiet experience of learning on their own to that of being in a lesson program. They enjoy the solitude, the more relaxed tempo, and the opportunities to experiment. Some like learning on their own because they're not good at taking another person's advice, and prefer to think they know better. Know which kind of person you are.

Decide if you and your horses are suitable candidates for a "self-study" approach. Some learning on one's own should be a part of any rider's program, if only to encourage independent thinking and self-confidence. But if your training résumé is short, or your horses are too green, or if you're trying to get somewhere in a hurry, you'd better take someone along with you.

And finally, recognize that taking that kind of journey alone in this sport can be a lonely experience at times. It's worth hearing from someone who sees it differently from you just to have someone to compare notes with at the end of the day. Besides, they might be right.

DON'T MAKE YOUR PROBLEM
YOUR TRAINER'S PROBLEM

Dear Janet: I read all your articles and especially like the ones about deal-ing with trainers. I am a nineteen-year-old jumper rider whose trainer is starting to build a good reputation for bringing along competitive horses and riders. I started with her last year and, at one show where I felt pushed, messed up pretty badly. I was miserable, my trainer was miser-able, and now I've backed off going to shows with her this year. I know that she, like most trainers, prefers her riders to do things a certain way at shows—for example, walk the course or warm up according to her meth-ods. I kind of like my ways but don't want to get on her bad side. How should I handle my trainer? I'm worried about being pushed at another show and getting yelled at again. —Liz

Liz, I can see exactly where the two of you are headed for a collision, unless you handle things differently. I can't advise you about han-dling your trainer because—sorry—it's not your place to handle her. This person is running her barn and program as she sees fit and, while I sometimes do discuss ways for students to ask more of their trainers or sensitize them to aspects of a program that aren't working, your predica-ment is a different story. Here's why.

First, you put yourself in training with someone who's known for making up competitive horses and riders and you want her to lay low at the in-gate?? No fair. Here's a parable for you: A hen asks a fox for help getting across the river. The fox assures safe passage, promising to be a gentleman. Halfway across the river the fox turns around, mouth wide open, ready to chomp. "What are you doing?!" exclaims the hen. "You promised me you wouldn't!"

"I'm a fox, you silly old hen. I do what foxes do."

Now, you and I and a whole bunch of other people may believe that pushing riders makes them try too hard and lose touch with their natural sensitivities. Most good riders are self-motivated anyway, and don't need pushing. But the whole bunch of others and I aren't your trainers. (You, I suspect, are trying to be your own co-trainer and that's another part of the problem, but more about that in a minute.) You picked your trainer, and it's not your place to ask this woman, who has spent years cultivating a business and style and reputation that *she* likes, to change. Decide instead if you want her training (and perhaps her pushing too, because these things are usually package deals) or not.

But wait a minute, and here's the second reason why yours is a different story. Did I really hear you say that you are "still uncertain about her way, and kind of like [your] ways"? Developing your own style is nice, but holy cow, girl—are you sure you really want a trainer? I'm not, and if I can't tell maybe your trainer can't either. People want to do the job they're hired for; hobbling your trainer with having to work around your "preferred" ways of preparing for a show and warming up can come off as provocative. Your trainer might correctly be recognizing this as "attitude." Either let this woman teach you, or move on.

OK, that said, Liz, here's what I'd suggest:

1. Decide if you can commit to a trainer's soup-to-nuts program at this point in your riding. You may do better as a ship-in student, which allows for greater independence. Remember that, in the end, you don't have to follow everything a person teaches you, but you *must be open in the beginning* or else you'll screen out things you think you don't need to learn about (which are usually the things you most need to learn about).

2. If you do commit, decide with the help of your parents and your current trainer whether her program is right for you. Ask your trainer if she feels you two are a good match. If she thinks not, ask her who she would recommend you work with instead.

3. If the fit is thought to be good, ask your trainer what she wants to see you doing differently in order to advance. Try to *soften* into the role of student, absorbing all you can from this person. Polite questions about differences in methods—*not as a way of saying how much you like your own way of doing things, but as a way of learning*—are OK; with this new game plan in place, you guys might be, too.

WHY CAN'T I LEARN MORE QUICKLY?

Dear Janet: I'm an obstetrician by day and a riding student come evening. All my life I've been a pretty quick study. I learn easily and put new ideas into action without much fuss. So what's with me and my riding lessons? My learning advances at the pace of a snail; the harder I work at it, the worse I get. I guess my question is just: "If I'm so smart, why do I feel so dumb?!" —Kathy

Kathy, I loved your letter and your obvious quest for excellence. But there are many reasons why even the most diligent student can find herself flummoxed by a seemingly sluggish rate of improvement. Some have to do with the nature of learning itself; others, with the nature of the learner.

What follows are some **common psychological obstacles** that crop up for riders in the lesson process. Not one is insurmountable. And because you'll know better than I which stumbling block has your name on it, I'll just lay them out. Look them over; if you find something relevant, work toward resolving it. Riding without stirrups and practicing gymnastics are wonderful for getting a leg up on skills, but I've always believed your best riding aid is your brain.

• **Perfectionism run amok!** The same attention to detail that probably helped you coast through medical school may be the culprit keeping you from grasping the bigger picture on horseback. There's nothing more destructive to a rider's natural sense of balance and rhythm and feel than trying to ride "perfectly" (whatever that means). Save perfect for the engineers, neurosurgeons, and air-traffic controllers. Go ahead and experiment with different decisions and positions and combinations of aids. Make mistakes. Figure out what works and what doesn't. Besides, your horse doesn't want to deal with a perfectionist any more than the rest of us do.

- **More important to be right than to be correct?** None of us think we do this . . . but haven't you had at least one argument where you (privately, silently) recognized you were being stubborn for the sake of not giving in?

The rider who wants more to be right than to be correct will (privately, silently) insist on "doing it her way" despite what the instructor is saying. "It" may be inconsequential to her riding progress, but her insistence creates a wall of secrecy and dries up the spongelike receptiveness a good student needs. Sneaking your foot a little farther into the stirrup, when your instructor isn't looking, is no match for asking her to help you feel more secure in the saddle.

- **Lingering loyalties.** Feeling loyal to a previous riding method or teacher—and fearing that trying another approach means compromising that loyalty—is a real dilemma. But the time to resolve it is before you put yourself into the hands of a new instructor. Otherwise, you're not being fair to yourself or her. You'll end up testing her, and she'll sense she's being tested. Moreover, your horse will sense your tentativeness in the way you give your aids. Decide beforehand what you're open to and what you're not. Then work toward stretching the former—and forget about proving your point.

- **Discomfort in the student role.** We grown-ups figure we've paid our schooling dues and are done having to listen to anyone tell us what to do. Some of us have worked hard to achieve positions where we can tell others what to do. So not every forty- or fifty-something is going to relish taking instruction from someone half his or her age. (High-powered professional and CEO types generally have the most difficulty being on the receiving end.) The more flexible you can be about changing roles, and the less you can view "studenthood" as an affront to your autonomy or intelligence, the better you'll be able to absorb the information being offered to you. Why go to the trouble of taking lessons just to show someone you don't need them?

MAKING THE MOST OF CLINICS

Dear Janet: After a successful show season, I felt ready to do a clinic with an expert nationally recognized for her excellent riding. I bought new riding clothes, spiffed up my horse, and told everybody about it for weeks.

At the clinic, the instructor immediately picked up on my riding problems. Even though she remained patient, the session went downhill from there. I told her I was having problems because I'd been taught a different method; consequently I froze, confusing my horse, who began pulling me around.

The second day was worse. Not only was my horse strong; he decided to be spooky. I could sense the expert's frustration as she repeated the same instruction over and over. I drove home feeling totally incompetent. Everything turned out so wrong—and my horse is still misbehaving, because now I'm so confused about which training methods to use. Why did I get such stage fright, and how can I ever feel comfortable going to another clinic? —Sharon

Sharon, how awful that your two clinic days turned out so miserably. Let me try to help you work your way out of your funk.

REGARDING THE CLINIC . . .

People go to clinics for different reasons: to learn new skills, sell a horse, impress the clinician, school over different terrain or new jumps, etc. You went to learn, and you prepared yourself and your horse well. But you got stuck when you tried to hang onto everything you already knew and ingest all the new stuff coming in.

What you need to do at clinics is soften your riding style enough to let the clinician shape you, not worrying so much about the way you usually do things. Later, with the help of your regular instructor or with the luxury of time, you can experiment and decide what new learnings to practice and keep, which to discard.

You did what a lot of clinic riders do: hurry to make everything they're learning immediately fit with what they've been taught, instead of taking their time to assimilate the information and blend it constructively with their existing riding style. Some riding questions can't get answered right away; prematurely answering them for the sake of closure results in frustration, not education.

REGARDING YOUR STAGE FRIGHT . . .

You probably got stage fright, Sharon, for the same reasons anyone gets it: *You wanted to do really well.* Whenever we try too hard, we don't ride as well as we do when we're not trying and just riding. Don't be hard on yourself for this; it's normal, if annoying. Either it'll go away with time and mileage or you'll learn to adapt to it by teaching yourself how to ride effectively even when you're feeling nervous.

REGARDING YOUR HORSE . . .

Sounds like you've become more worried about doing "the right thing" than about doing *some* thing. Settle back into the way you'd been riding; then gradually reintroduce new techniques or concepts from the clinic. Don't try to change everything at once. It's one thing to have a clinician significantly modify your riding for one or two days under her supervision; it's quite another to carry out the change on your own. Your horse will settle down when you begin communicating and reacting to him with some degree of confidence and authority again.

And, finally . . .

REGARDING GOING TO OTHER CLINICS . . .

You go, Sharon! You are as good a rider as you were before this clinic, just confused. More important, you have the makings of a good clinic student: You took the instruction graciously, without overpersonalizing or becoming defensive toward the instructor. Yes, you got frustrated, but it sounds as if you kept that to yourself. (It's possible, too, if the clinician hasn't taught much, that she was limited in her ability to manage a teaching snafu.)

When you attend other clinics, bear in mind that some clinicians get visibly (and vocally) impatient or unduly critical during sessions. Many clinics are part education and part theater. Don't take the drama personally; just soak up all the learning you can.

DON'T GET FRUSTRATED, GET GOING!

arah wants to know what to do when her training troubles get the best of her: *I was wondering if you had any suggestions on how to deal with frustration toward yourself and your horse when every other day he takes two steps back in his training. At the end of some days, I wind up just sitting in my horse's stall crying while he dumps hay in my hair. I'm not asking to go from Training Level to Second in a year, but doing Training Level one month and less than Intro the next is weighing down my spirits. I'm a positive person, but I've dealt with this for more than two years, and it's getting old.*

I have several thoughts after reading your letter, Sarah.

• **First, reconsider your program.** You need a program that works a whole lot better for you than the one you've got. Chronic backward movement in your horse's progress is a pretty clear sign that something's not right. If you don't already *have* a program, that might be where to begin. Vague goals, loose timelines, erratic training schedules, too few guidelines for knowing when a horse is ready to master the next step, and insufficient professional input all point to a horse-and-rider combo that isn't going to get the job done.

Start by identifying—with help from an excellent trainer or knowledgeable friend—the specific problems that are causing you and your horse to regress. Are they related to readiness for the work you're doing, soundness, conformation, his attitude, your attitude, your education? Is he a bully? A worrier? A spook? Are you?

I've always thought that the best riders have as keen a knack for diagnostics as for their riding. I think you need to refine your analysis of the problem. If you don't, you'll end up with vague or (worse) inappropriate solutions that won't work. Or you might fall into the other miserable trap:

desperately applying all sorts of gadgetry that doesn't teach you how to ride effectively through your aids. So go back to the barn, sit on a stump, and take your time to study the problem as thoroughly as you're capable of doing.

• **Second . . . sorry, but I'm going to tell you to reconsider your attitude.** The best students of any sport have always been those who've looked at themselves first when trying to locate the source of training or performance trouble. You'll do much better, Sarah, once you adopt a more proactive approach to solving this problem with your horse. That means assuming the initiative for change, rather than only reacting to what he is or isn't doing.

To your credit, you don't spend your time pointing fingers—as some very disappointed riders do. But you need to be more focused and honest with yourself about weak spots and holes in your riding, so that you can move the process along. I know your results have been very discouraging, but keep that positive perspective you spoke of and use it to help you jump-start the program your horse needs.

• **Third, use your frustration constructively.** Feeling frustrated, even talking about it with others, becomes something constructive instead of draining when you use it to make something different happen in your riding life. If you're disgusted with your horse because he doesn't "get it," or because he was round on Tuesday but hollow on Thursday when your friends came to watch, keep your disgust to yourself and think about how *you* might have ridden differently on those two days.

Read more. Consult more. Watch more. Sulk less. The more you can manage to view these stumbling blocks as growth-promoting challenges, rather than as disillusionment or dashed hopes, the further you'll go. Learning to be an excellent student of this sport is the most important riding lesson you'll ever get.

HE'S TOO GOOD FOR ME

This is not about boyfriends, fiancés, or husbands. This is about horses—horses whose owners worry about being good enough for, or *worthy of*, their nice, talented equine partners.

Judy found she was feeling exceptionally nervous before each horse show, for reasons she couldn't quite figure out. She liked doing well but was not hell-bent on winning. She didn't give a hoot what the folks standing by the rail thought about her, and she felt confident about her selection of classes and degree of preparation. All systems go, right?

You'd think so. But the problem was that Judy believed she owed her guy a good ride, one commensurate with his talent. Which really meant a great ride, one through which he could, ahem, *self-actualize* his potential.

Did anybody here take an Intro to Psych class? Remember the professor drawing that pyramid on the board—the one with the words "safety" and "food" and "shelter" on the bottom, and "self-actualization" at the tippy-top? That was Abraham Maslow's pyramid of human needs and potentials, illustrating his idea that we humans can best self-actualize—free our self-expression, creativity, and achievement—only when we've met our fundamental needs. This means no one can achieve his or her potential as a craftsperson, parent, dancer, writer, or athlete if he or she is worried about paying the mortgage, securing adequate food supplies, or protecting loved ones from harm.

Sadly, most human beings on this earth aren't ever really free enough from the day-to-day challenges of making their lives work that they feel the urge to "self-actualize" on any kind of regular basis. A widowed mother in Romania who's worrying about finding a kiosk with fresh bread and vegetables for her kids doesn't think much about her untrained and undiscovered lovely voice. A young Triple-A ballplayer whose father's health is failing is too concerned about both his parents' welfare to play the way he otherwise might and finally break into the big leagues. . . .

But Maslow drew his pyramid to represent human needs, not horses'. And when we anthropomorphize our equine partners—envision them with human needs and feelings about achieving potentials—we lose the uniqueness of both their species and our own . . . and the sheer, simple fun of enjoying them.

What Judy feels isn't uncommon. She's in the company of thousands of other riders who worry about failing or having failed their horses by not having been able to give them a good enough ride. "You talk about your horse as if you feel you betrayed him," I tell her. "I do, I do!" she replies. "He's *such* a nice horse. He could go far!"

I suppose Judy's horse could go far. Maybe he will, maybe not. But the fact of the matter is that he's got other things on his mind. Horse things. Like what that rustle is in the leaves, and whether the grass is better over there, and whether there's grain in his bucket when he comes in from being turned out. He knows nothing about year-end finals and can't distinguish the word "Devon" from the term "sheath-cleaning."

That *we* have dreams and want to go far is terrific. That our horses do, well, I don't know. There are those horses who love the limelight, and some who won't let themselves be retired, but that's something different. We need to content ourselves with being able to give our horses a fair ride, a kind and intelligent one. That's a good ride. That's what we owe them. We betray them only when we strip them of their nature as horses who, by virtue of biological destiny, instinctively concern themselves with life's more fundamental affairs: safety, food, shelter.

Were they to understand more, maybe they would envy our capacities for enjoying achievement and mastery. Maybe that's what's different about those few special ones who light up as they enter the ring. But we can envy them, too. We can envy our horses the simplicity they have without being simple creatures, as well as their displays of grace and contentedness with the smaller pleasures in life that you or I might take for granted—a warm, dry bed, a midafternoon snack, a pat on the shoulder.

ARE YOU TOO NICE?

W e've all witnessed something like this: Rider on a trail walks her horse over toward the remaining sliver of an almost-defunct creek, lets him decide how he wants to handle it, and waits. He, in turn, decides to handle it as would—surprise!—a horse: He swivels and runs back to the barn. Rider leans down, pats him, and starts over again.

Despite what your mother told you, there is such a thing as being too nice, and this is a good example. What else do "too nice" riders do? They worry about upsetting their horses with too much work. They worry that their horses won't like the weather. They worry about their horses worrying. If their horses were teen-aged children, these riders would be asking them if they liked their 11:00 p.m. curfew or would prefer a later one.

WHAT'S WRONG WITH NICE?

So what's the big deal, you wonder. Can't this world use some more nice in it? Well, sure. But nice itself was never the problem. Nice run amok is.

Look what happens with our teenagers when nice takes a free-fall: "Ma, how about 4:00 a.m. for my curfew? I think I could work with that. And you don't mind if I take your car, do you? It's a whole lot cleaner than mine."

It's not so different with horses. They may not be actively looking to put one over on you, but they'll take the freebie offered their way: "Oh, I get to decide when to start listening to your aids? Sure—in a minute, after I sniff the cows in the next field. Be right with you!"

There's more: Being too nice around horses can be dangerous. People sometimes get kicked, bitten, dumped, and run off with precisely because they aren't good at saying "No!" Being nice has never been reliable protection against being taken advantage of.

AT SECOND BLUSH

Nice people are often genuinely nice people. They come that way. But every so often, being too nice masquerades for something else. Some people—especially some women—have been brought up believing that being authoritative is not acceptable; that it's ill-mannered, pushy, or unfeminine. Such a person avoids all self-assertion and never feels comfortable speaking up for herself. She grows up to be—well, too nice.

Many people who act too nice are "mistake-o-phobics." Mistake-o-phobics spend their days chasing the cruel, elusive dream of being perfect. They think no one will ever get mad at them for their mistakes as long as they are nice.

And some people are mild-mannered by temperament. Their niceness hides nothing. It's their own gentle way.

BEING NICE "ENOUGH"

Want to adjust your nice-o-meter without feeling like an ogre?

First, to get your horse to respect your wishes, you need to be committed to your requests. Use your riding aids clearly and definitely. If you want him to pay more attention to you than to those cows, tell him and mean it. This is not unkind. Your horse will still be your friend. He won't complain about you over the water trough later.

Second, to be committed, you need to know your horse can deliver the goods. Only then can you decisively ask him for collection, or adjustability between fences, or long periods of attention. Ask a trainer or knowledgeable friend to gauge his potential if you're not sure.

Third, remember that horses are herd animals. They like leadership in their handlers. They seek and rely on guidance from you. Your telling them what to do doesn't burden them; it supports them.

Fourth, learn that you're entitled to ask your horse to work for you. I often have to tell a "too nice" client that her horse is very well cared for and that it is OK for her to take an hour or so each day to "borrow" him for herself!

Still having trouble exiting the "too nice" state? Do what Gina did. Gina came to me searching for a way to remember to "be the boss" with her new, rather strong-willed horse. Given her affinity for things "regal" and her wish to balance authority with compassion, I suggested she put on her horse's stall door the King of Hearts from a deck of cards: a visual trigger for her desired attitude. A "king of hearts" Gina became.

COOLIN' IT

An insightful man writes in to ask how he can better control his temper while riding. "Eric" says he occasionally succumbs to brief bouts of raw anger during which he punishes his horse for disobediences with the stick or bit. He doesn't like having these fits, and he recognizes they gratify a part of him that likes exerting control over another. He also recognizes that most horses' problems and disobediences are "direct results of rider faults." Eric does manage to keep his anger in check when other people are around, but not riding alone. He asks, *"How can I stop these anger episodes?"*

For openers, Eric, I applaud your candor and your search for a way of dealing with your temper. We've all been exposed to riders' tantrums on horseback, from the short-stirrup kids on up through the professional ranks. It's nice to see someone take responsibility for his actions, rather than blaming his horse/trainer/groom/mother/early childhood, and take active steps to change, too.

I've come up with three levels of intervention you can consider, each a little more complex than the one before.

The first level involves a conscious effort to separate the feelings of wanting to control or punish from the action of doing so. We're not responsible for *how* we feel—we're not in control of that—only for what we *do* with our feelings. Use your self-awareness to *drive a wedge between thought and action,* stopping yourself as soon as you feel yourself shifting toward aggressiveness.

The second level involves trying some specific mental strategies to stop a temper flare-up or to preempt it altogether.

• **Call up the psychological resources you already have.** What is it you're able to do, say to yourself, inhibit yourself from doing when riding with others? What you need to do when riding alone, then, is not developing self-control from scratch, but applying in a different context the self-control you have inside.

• **Interrupt the standard pattern of response.** If someone desperately wanted to stop biting her nails, I might suggest she look at each nail before chomping and tenderly say goodbye to it. While she's yielding to the urge to bite, she's already begun to change her habit's pattern. Changing a habit is a powerful precursor to ending it; it breaks the integrity of what had been an automatic, reflexive behavior. Thus, make yourself apologize to your horse before doing anything inappropriate until you become so aware of your actions that you can stop them. Or commit to singing four bars of "Edelweiss" before you react, or taking your feet out of your stirrups—anything to change what you customarily do.

• **Resurrect the power of heroes.** When I want to inspire myself toward acts of integrity and moral courage, I think of Atticus Finch, attorney-hero of Harper Lee's *To Kill a Mockingbird*. When you start feeling the urge to punish your horse, conjure up an image of someone from the riding community whom you respect. Visualize this person handling the very situation you're dealing with. Better than visualizing this, put yourself in that person's body and *become* him or her. Remember in the movie *Ghost* how Patrick Swayze's character took over Whoopi Goldberg's body so he could dance with his wife? Like that.

• **Gratify the impulse to control by controlling your temper, rather than your horse.** A little mental gymnastics here does the trick. Did you know that many people purposefully put themselves in tempting situations, where *not* letting themselves do what they're tempted to do feels powerful to them, and good? This is not weird, just one more slant to our multifaceted human nature.

If these strategies don't work for you, Eric, you may need to move to a third level of intervention, such as avoiding riding alone, riding only under a trainer's supervision, or examining in psychotherapy why you're displacing such anger onto your horse. Sometimes, when a person treats another in such a harsh way, it's because he or she was once the recipient of such treatment. Were that true in your case, Eric, you would be like so many others who try to master an emotional pain by turning it around and perpetuating it. Often, if such a person can develop compassion for his own earlier trials, he becomes able to extend that compassion to others.

WHERE'S THE ACTION?

A lonely rider writes: *Two years ago, my horse and I moved from a busy show barn to a private barn with one other boarder. I basically have no riding companions and have not been riding my aged equine partner as much. I could never give it up, but I do not feel as inspired as when I was going to shows and had companions. Does my slump mean I am not truly devoted to the sport? Why do I feel so bored? —Caroline*

Caroline, I'm about as devoted and inspired as they come, but put me in a two-stall barn with no riding buddies and I go catatonic. It just wouldn't work for me, and I imagine it just doesn't work for you. We can compensate for a lot of missing pieces in our riding programs through mental effort and pep talks, but we all have particular environments that make us tick and others that leave us cold.

There are many riders who function and train and feel their best at low-key facilities where they have opportunities to practice unobserved, move around unself-consciously, and get respite from human contact and conversation. They don't enjoy the hustle and bustle of a busy show barn, or maybe they get distracted by all the goings-on. They may be much happier in a smaller, quieter barn where they can work toward their competitive or schooling goals privately, or where they share noncompetitive riding interests with other boarders.

And then there are the others, like me and probably you, who thrive in a livelier, more social, more competitive environment. You mentioned missing horse shows? Well, stick a horse show at the end of *my* week and I'm on fire Monday through Friday. What can I say? I'm a horse-show animal. Maybe you are, too.

Don't worry that your slump means there's some big problem in you as a rider. What seems more probable is that you changed your riding environment and it turned out not to be your cup of tea. Here are some ideas for how you can get back on track again.

- **If possible, consider returning to your old barn or one like it.** If you can't . . .

- **You don't mention whether or not you're still training,** but what about bringing an instructor out to your barn on a regular basis so you have that to look forward to? It will also help you practice on the days you ride by yourself. Use the lesson features in *Practical Horseman* and other magazines to supplement your training and don't forget about attending clinics as well.

- **Talk to other riders, amateur and professional,** who ride in similar settings. How do they keep the doldrums away?

- **Reformulate your goals to better match your current situation,** even if it is temporary. If you are still showing, pull together a game plan for the season. You may need to change divisions, scout out horse shows on your own, arrange your own shipping, find a trainer who can help you at shows, and so on. If showing isn't feasible right now, consider other activities, such as Pony Club (you didn't mention your age) or an adult horse group (check the calendar in local horse publications for names and meeting dates), gymkhanas, hunter paces, competitive or pleasure trail riding and the like.

- **And finally, try to create as much of that social and show-barn atmosphere on your own as you can.** Dress well when you ride, have a riding/training goal for the day, hang up a radio to punch out some good music, groom your horse as if you're going somewhere, collect your prize lists or clinic brochures and post them, stick a big calendar on the wall of the barn with a monthly plan, and so on. Invite a friend out for an afternoon to hang out with you. Model your own horse management after those qualities you admire in a well-run show barn—you might be surprised at how much mileage you get out of that in terms of both attitude and outlook.

Not to worry, Caroline—you're not any less serious or less devoted than you were before. You've just lost your bearings a little, and you're in a physical place that doesn't work well for your psychological needs. The boredom, the slump will evaporate when you find a riding environment that fans your flames of interest. Once the ball is rolling again, it should feel just like old times.

WANT TO RIDE BETTER?
WIDEN YOUR WORLD

Years (and years) ago, when I first popped my head out of graduate school, I asked a colleague for recommendations on professional readings. Current events, he said. The performing arts. Maybe languages. Definitely sports and music.

Really? I said. What about books on diagnosing and family-systems theory? What about current advances in research?

You'll read that anyway, Jed predicted. Don't put the other stuff off until you have "more time." You'll never have it. Read anything that makes you a better human being, and you'll become a better psychologist.

He was right.

I'll take it a step further. I figure too that the same things making you a better, more well-rounded human being help you to become a better rider.

In my practice, I recently saw a dressage enthusiast who'd gotten herself in a bind over "correct" position. The harder she tried to recover her sense of "correctness," the more rigid and contrived her position became; soon she could hardly tell her right from her left. Her horse did the only reasonable thing he could in such a situation: He got really stiff.

Darcy needed a different way out of this jam: something other than doing more of the same and trying harder. She needed to study not technique, but fluidity, loss of self-consciousness, kinesthetics. I sent her to a yoga class.

Young Courtney was having a problem with her pony—or so she believed. Since the onset of a summer slump, she'd been out of the good ribbons and, increasingly, out of good spirits. The harder she tried to ride perfect hunter rounds, the more elusive they became. Her pony protested with tension. She blamed the problem on him.

Courtney practiced more jumping lines, took more lessons, and swore to herself to do it more perfectly the next time. She came to me for help getting that perfect round. I told her I could help her get it if she first learned to be a better partner to her pony. I also told her that she needed to find room in her program for the slumps, dumps, lumps, and bumps that go along with any serious sport training, and that developing these parts of herself—patience, tolerance, accountability, and partnership—would be infinitely more valuable than a thousand practice jumps.

I was right.

Sometimes the shortest route between two points is not a straight line.

The psychologists I know who wound up studying only books on diagnosis and research are boring. They use too many empty techniques in their work and not enough of their own wisdom. They are only marginally effective at helping people change and feel better.

The next time you find yourself pumping away furiously at a solution that is offering less and less hope, stop. It may be the wrong solution, the wrong time, the wrong way. Do something different. Get fresh ideas from a friend, a customer, a grandma.

Believe it or not, those other people don't have to know about riding horses. Sometimes it's better that they don't. Sometimes the problem isn't a riding problem, just as it wasn't for Courtney. If you are brave enough, and if you are serious enough about your riding, ask those people what they think is the one thing you need to do more of or less of to become a better athlete. Then sit back and listen to what they say.

Here's something else you can do. In your tack trunk, keep a copy of this poem (a favorite of psychologist Carl Rogers, it's by a nineteenth-century author, Mrs. Edward Craster):

> *The centipede was happy quite*
> *Until the toad in fun*
> *Said, "Pray, which leg goes after*
> *which?"*
> *And worked her mind to such a*
> *pitch,*
> *She lay distracted in the ditch,*
> *Considering how to run.*

A SPORT OF SEEMING OPPOSITES

Dear Janet: Help! I don't get it. During lessons, my trainer tells me to do one thing, then another that seems like the opposite. Last week, for example, she was helping me find good distances to fences with my schooling jumper; then she told me not to help him so much when we came to the fence but let him figure it out for himself. Today she was telling me to stay loose and more relaxed in my tack but also to ride more aggressively, as if I'm the boss. I'm confused. I feel as if the instructions cancel each other out! Can't someone just tell me what to do? —Ally

Up to a point, Ally. First, though, you've got to make sure that you understand each individual instruction. For instance, can you distinguish between the different distances your instructor is asking you to find, and tell when one suits better than another? Do you understand what she means by telling you to encourage your horse to jump the fence himself, and how that differs from dropping him in front of a fence?

Riding is, in many ways, a puzzle to be solved. And as with any puzzle, finding the solution will be next to impossible if any pieces are missing. Your understanding is one big piece of that puzzle. So the first step for you is to take more responsibility and ask your trainer to clarify points you're not sure about.

But even with that piece in place, some aspects of the riding puzzle will become clear only after you've spent time alone with them, both in your mind and on your horse. That's where riders discover the way out of the paradoxes. Maybe the two instructions—to ride aggressively and to stay relaxed, for example—aren't opposites. Maybe they are *conditional* opposites: If your horse does A, you do B. If he does B, you do A. Maybe you just don't get it yet. That's OK, too. Maybe anything. Don't take offense at the sport's complexities; take your time.

Read on, Ally, for additional ideas on making the most out of your education:

- **Ask yourself if you feel resentful about being a student.** Having someone teach you something new is not insulting to your intelligence or riding ability or station in life. It's enviable. I still envy college students whose primary job is to learn; I wish I could do it all over again.

- **Learn to ask good questions that help you better understand each part of the puzzle.** One example: "Kathy, how do I determine whether to help my horse out over a jump or let him figure it out more on his own? How do I make that decision?" Another: "Whenever I try to ride aggressively, I get tense. What do I need to do differently?" The best "askers" are open, candid, forthright, inquisitive, clear. The worst are defensive, challenging, and provocative. Their questions have an edge; they come with "attitude."

Your trainer should be able (and willing) to respond with information that elaborates upon and clarifies earlier instructions. But you must also accept that at some point there may be no more answers to be given; the rest of your learning must come from your own thinking things through and trying ideas out.

- **Be absolutely sure you've picked an instructor whom you trust.** This is essential, because it allows you to take in all the information she offers. Later you can sort out that information and categorize and question. The time for critical thinking is after you've gathered as much data as possible; if you screen and make judgments "at the door," a lot of good stuff gets left behind.

- **Learn to view the puzzles of riding as challenges rather than obstacles.** Doing so will make an enormous difference in your riding, and in the quality of your relationship with the sport. No one is trying to trick you; no one is trying to make you work extra hard; no one is trying to hold you back. This sport is complex. Unless you accept that fact, you will pay an enormous price in terms of exasperation and impatience and discouragement. You'll feel inadequate. You'll feel unathletic. You'll feel stupid.

You are none of those things. You are an evolving rider. Be more tolerant of the process of learning and you will feel better about yourself, your horse, and your relationship with your instructor.

[CHAPTER 4]

Relationships, Conflicts, Jealousies, and Sportsmanship

HOW COME YOU DON'T KNOW
WHAT I'M THINKING?

Everybody wants a mind reader—for a husband, wife, friend, business partner, therapist, student, teacher. . . . When these people turn out *not* to be mind readers, we get disappointed; sometimes we get angry. "You should know," we say to them under our breath—or "You *should have* known" and (for good measure) "you better know next time."

Well, we could wait forever for others to guess that we have something we want them to know about, let alone guess it correctly. Some people do wait forever, committed to their silence. They become resentful, feel misunderstood, get self-righteous. Hollow triumphs, all.

Riders tell me their trainers don't understand their needs. Trainers, too, tell me they don't understand their riders' needs, or that they do but don't understand why their riders aren't learning. Are these riders telling their trainers what they need? No. Are their trainers asking? No. Everyone wants it all to happen without discussion. What, it should work by osmosis?

So riders clam up, or they convince themselves that everything's OK or that that's all you can expect from life anyway. Trainers do the same, or they just label the student as one who "doesn't listen" or "gives into her fears too easily" or "doesn't take his riding seriously enough."

Talking about things doesn't have to be such a big deal. It doesn't have to be "deep" or "serious" or "long." It just has to be honest to your experience of riding and training at that time. Consider the following ideas for making your communication as effective as possible:

• **Bring up your concerns early, while they're still just an idea or thought you have about something, rather than a "problem."** If you're concerned that your trainer is taking too long to sell your horse, ask her what her ideas are for a next step. Should you put some more ads in the papers and horse journals? Should you lower the asking price? How does she typically handle the selling of a slow-moving horse? Don't grumble under your breath that nothing's happening.

- **Think out ahead of time exactly what it is you want to communicate.** Keep it simple so your trainer has a good shot at understanding precisely what you mean to say.

"Listen, Rich, I want to talk with you sometime soon about my lesson program. I've been feeling ready to move up a level, but I don't get the sense that you necessarily think so."

"I know you've been trying to help me, Joan, but when you yell at me in the schooling area at shows, I feel really embarrassed and lose my concentration."

- **Add a comment about how you feel bringing up your concern, if doing so is difficult or anxiety-provoking. It really helps.**

"I feel a little nervous telling you this—because the last time I brought this up with a trainer, she felt challenged, and that wasn't what I intended. . . . "

"I'm worried you'll think I'm a big chicken if I tell you how afraid I've become, but I don't see any way around it. . . . It's important to me; I hope you understand. . . . "

- **Try to describe to your trainer exactly what you want to have done differently.** Offer a specific vision of what you want, so that you present yourself as an active part of the change process and not just a complainer.

Tell your trainer what you need more or less of, and at what times (e.g., more support by the in-gate, more constructive criticism during lessons, a more candid appraisal of the suitability of your horse for you).

Also, tell your trainer—without blaming—what *doesn't* work so well for you. Some strategies function terrifically with some students and backfire with others. Your trainer may simply not have picked up—and maybe you haven't been sending—any recognizable sign that a particular way of communicating or teaching is not effective for you. You could go on for years that way. Don't. Commit to securing something better for yourself. The burden is yours, though. Wish as we might, thoughts stay just thoughts.

ADDRESSING SAFETY HAZARDS

Dear Janet: I keep my horse in a small, private barn where four of us gals take care of our own horses. For the most part it works and we get along, but one person, Gail, is new to horsekeeping and makes some big mistakes. The other day she turned her horse out without "bothering" to put a lead shank on for the walk out to the paddocks. I've also observed her removing blankets by opening all of the front buckles before undoing the belly straps. Just yesterday she left her horse crosstied to his bit! "Oh, it was just for a second," she said when she saw my eyes bug out. What can I try saying to her that will get her to be more careful without making her more defensive? —Kay

Kay, I can't promise that anything I suggest will keep Gail's hackles down but the risks are so high you'll need to plug on anyway. Here are some things to try:

Approach her unapologetically but without an agenda of Proving A Point (i.e., that she doesn't know what she's doing). "Gail," you could say, "I need to talk with you about some safety points around the barn and I'm hoping you won't feel offended. I'm just worried that you or the horses could get hurt." Explain to her that surcingles can become bucking straps when the front buckles are released first and how easy it is for a spooked or stumbling horse to get away from a handler who isn't using a lead. When you notice her making other mistakes, calmly point it out on the spot, explain why it's unsafe, and tell her what to do instead. Don't get angry—educate. If either of you gets an attitude, the situation will deteriorate into a miserable control battle.

If that happens, re-approach the problem by addressing the tension that's developed between the two of you. "Gail, I don't want this to become an awkward situation for us and I can see we're already uncomfortable. I don't mean for you to feel criticized or unknowledge-able. I really only want for you and us and the horses not to get hurt. Can we try this again?"

Be careful, Kay, not to sound like a know-it-all, and make sure to distinguish between practices that you prefer she do (because you like them done that way) and those that you need her to do (for safety reasons).

Hope that helps. While we're at it, here are some suggestions for two other popular barn blunders you (and other readers) are bound to see.

You're a guest at a friend's barn, there to ride her new horse. You know nobody, nobody knows you, but you notice a guy grazing his horse. Uh-oh, you also notice the guy doubled the chain through the halter loop, leaving a inviting ring of metal for his horse's foot to go through whenever he drops his head. What do you say?

"You know, I don't mean to disturb you but I once heard of a horse putting his foot right through the loop in the chain on the halter. Poor thing panicked and pulled his foot right off. Hope you didn't mind my two cents, but that ugly story is pasted to my memory bank."

Trainer Fran throws a horse's halter on in the stall but leaves the throatlatch open while picking out his feet, and tacking him up. He stays like that for the few minutes she goes to get his bridle, put on her chaps, chat with a friend. She leads him out by holding on to the loose cavesson. She's been lucky so far—no loose, swinging halter straps getting caught on hooks or poking into eyes. But what rider wants to count on luck?

This is a tricky one; Fran probably owns or at least runs the facil-ity. She doesn't want to hear from boarders that they don't like her horse handling. Telling Fran a story (like with the grazer before), about what you once saw or heard happen will probably make your suggestion more palatable than trying to be a 'do-gooder': "Hey Fran, remember that guy, Dave, from Happiest Horse Farm? He used to tack up with an open hal-ter until the day his steady-eddie horse got the throatlatch caught on the salt lick. Well, steady-eddie freaked and put a gash in his head the size of the Panama Canal. Dave doesn't do that anymore. Just a thought."

An unfortunate truth about many handlers is that they're hard to advise. They "already know" the correct way (which really means *their* way), and don't want help, don't need it. Unfortunately, the horses sometimes tell a different story.

WHEN TRAINER AND
BARN MANAGER SPLIT

Dear Janet: I've been going to the same barn for ten years. Now the barn manager and trainer, both excellent, are splitting up. The manager will stay at my current barn, and my trainer is setting up a new barn; both are asking the boarders to make a choice between them. It feels like a divorce!

I'm having a terrible time choosing—I'm not sure how well either would cover the other person's role. I can count on the barn manager to check on any horse problems I have, and to be there any day my horse needs the vet or farrier. My trainer knows how to get the best out of my horse and me, and she'll have better turnout, but I'm not sure I can count on her being there every day to look after my horse. She's on the road a lot, showing a lot, including Florida, for six weeks each winter; I don't know who she'll be leaving at the barn to run things in her absence.

When I ask the manager and trainer questions about their new arrangements, they each say they don't have all the answers yet. For the time being, I've stayed at my current barn—but most of the other boarders have moved with our trainer, so I feel I've lost my social environment. I can't make a decision! What's wrong with me?! —Ellen

Nothing's wrong with you, Ellen. You're circumspect and patient in your decision-making. This is not a simple matter of, "Do I buy the blue saddle pad or the plaid one?" This is, "Where is my riding future going to be best realized?" So take your time to think it through.

Probably the best thing about your situation is that you don't have to decide anything by yesterday. Your former fellow boarders can always do reconnaissance for you at your trainer's new barn (providing there are no hard feelings between them and you). And you can continue periodically to ask questions of the barn manager and trainer as their new circumstances evolve more clearly.

One way to begin sorting things out is to identify the aspects of care and training that are most important to you. Some barn managers are absolutely irreplaceable, but in most cases a trainer can replace a manager more easily than a manager can replace a seasoned trainer. However, if work and family obligations mean you're not able to be "on call" for vet and farrier appointments, you'll need a barn with someone available to do that for you. That means you probably need to stay put until your trainer has that piece in place—which, given her show schedule, will likely be soon.

You intimated that the barn manager would be taking over training responsibilities at your current barn. Does she have experience doing that, or is she planning to wing it? Any chance you could ship in to your trainer's new barn for lessons without precipitating another Cold War?

Yes, it can feel like a divorce—two caretakers in whom you have faith, who've functioned under one roof, deciding to go their separate ways. It will surely feel that way if divorce has been part of your own past; this current scenario can rekindle all kinds of funky feelings that may shadow your present decision-making. Such a history might even explain why you're having trouble committing to one over the other, if having done so in the past (even if the decision was made for you by the custodial parent) resulted in bad feelings and messy relations.

Everybody reacts differently to change, Ellen, and you'll eventually figure out where your home should be. Some people are comfortable making swift moves in the face of choices; others need more time. As long as no one is being unduly held up by your contemplations, take your time inquiring about and evaluating the management and training styles at the two barns. Be careful, though, not to put the burden on the manager and trainer to "prove" themselves to you; you could come off as annoying or condescending.

Think outside the box, too: Is there another barn you've always been curious about but never had an excuse to explore? "Change" can morph into "opportunity" more quickly than horses spook.

GETTING YOUR STUFF BACK

Dear Janet: I board at a barn where everybody gets along pretty well and there's a lot of borrowing of equipment. Most of the time stuff gets put back in its place, or it can be tracked down easily enough.

My problem is that I don't really like lending my stuff out all the time. I don't mind someone occasionally asking to borrow my draw reins or a bit, but it's gotten so casual that people are starting to "forget" to ask; they just assume it's OK because it was OK the last time. Nobody else seems to mind this, but I'm finding it really annoying.

Another problem: My stuff is a lot nicer than everyone else's, and I take better care of it. When someone borrows my tack and returns it dirty, I'm so amazed and so angry that I'm afraid anything I say will be something I'll regret—so I just don't say anything.

One more thing: This one girl's had one of my bits for weeks. How do I ask her to give it back without getting her mad?

Can you help me out? I love everything else at my barn, so please don't tell me to leave! —Chris

All right, Chris, I won't tell you to leave. But the rest of my advice won't be any walk in the park. First of all, if borrowing/sharing/lending/forgetting is the accepted culture in this barn, give up any idea of getting the other boarders to change. You're outnumbered, and you ain't got veto power.

So you're left having either to ride this river in the direction it flows (which I don't advise because I think you'll soon be miserable) or to set some personal limits—and to somehow communicate them in a way that makes the other boarders not roll their eyes at your perceived "fussiness" (note, I said perceived) but oblige your preference for order and organization.

Best way to do that?

- **Appreciate that there are multiple perspectives.** Recognize that some people like the system of "what's yours is mine and what's mine is yours." It's not your way, but it doesn't have to be. Make sure your fellow boarders know you appreciate this, or they'll think you're being too judgmental.

- **Use first-strike humor.** Find some way to poke gentle fun at yourself when you explain you'd prefer not to swap equipment around: "I'm sorry, guys, but not knowing where my stuff is turns me into such a worrywart it's ridiculous. Would you mind if I just kept my stuff to myself for the most part? What can I say? Hey, at least you don't have to LIVE with me!" If you don't tease yourself, they'll do it for you—when you're not around.

- **Remain flexible.** "Hey, listen, guys, if there's anything you ever really need, don't count me out. Just please be sure to ask me first. I'm sure I'll want to help." This lets them know it's not so black-and-white that they can't ever ask you for a favor. If you come off as entirely unapproachable, everybody will be miserable and your stabling there will have become a gross mismatch.

Oh, yeah: Forget about getting anything returned clean. Cleaning the tack you borrow is such an obvious courtesy that if you have to start educating your fellow boarders about it, they're going to start calling you "Miss Manners." It's not worth the hassle.

As for the girl with your bit, keep it simple and low-key. You don't need a reason, excuse, or apology to ask for your bit back, just words like "Hey, you got that slow-twist I lent you the other week? Just trying to pull my stuff together. If you like it, I know they have them at HappyHorse Tack Shop." If that kind of request makes her mad, then she has more problems than you can protect her from by mincing your words. You are doing nothing wrong by asking for your things back. Just don't throw your earlier generosity in her face, or you'll have her growling at you under her breath.

BAD SPORT KID

Dr. Edgette, I never thought I'd be in this situation but I am. My thirteen-year-old daughter has been riding and showing for a couple of years now. She's an excellent rider but a terrible sport. She doesn't mean to be, and says she can't help it when she feels bad. But whenever she does poorly, she'll come out of the ring crying and snap at her trainer or at me. Once or twice I've seen her hit her pony with a stick walking him back to the trailer. I've tried talking to her and she says she's trying, but I don't see any difference in her attitude and now she's starting to get defensive whenever her father or I bring the topic up. I hate to have to "punish" her—she's otherwise a great kid—but I can't seem to get the point across that she's too big to act so childish. Can you help us? —Margaret

Margaret, if ever there was a letter right up my alley this one is it. For a while I've been lamenting the evaporating sense of personal accountability on the part of young people, both in and out of sport circles. Your struggles with your daughter give me the perfect opportunity to address the issue right here in this column.

What you and your husband are witnessing in your daughter is her mistaken belief that because feelings can't be controlled, neither can behaviors. This is not true, and she needs you and her father to emphasize this to her, on every occasion in which she declines to see her actions as matters of choice.

Yes, children and adults alike get overwhelmed and have trouble staying calm or rational. But it's folly to view her unsportsmanlike behavior and attitudes as beyond her control. She indulges herself at the show because she gets away with it, and because she's not yet been forced to find more appropriate ways to handle frustration. Kids who scream at their trainers and make snide remarks to their parents and blame their ponies for poor performances will never learn to feel responsible for the events in their lives, good or bad.

Your daughter needs help so that she doesn't continue to indulge her temper or her expectations that what she wants—no matter how hard she has worked for it—is something she necessarily gets. This is a lesson much better learned now, at home with people who love her and know her kinder side, than later, with people who will simply react. Here are some specific ways to guide her:

Together with your husband, tell your daughter that you have become increasingly concerned about her poor behavior and attitudes. Explain that your addressing it with patience and understanding has not been effective enough in getting her to change it. Tell her that because of this, you will have clear expectations about what she can and cannot say and do at shows, and that if she feels unable to cooperate, you are prepared to suspend some of her riding privileges.

Next, outline to your daughter your expectations, e.g., no hitting her pony, no talking back to trainers, parents, or any other adults, no abusive or rude comments to anyone, peers included. Let her know that you and your husband will always be willing to address and discuss legitimate questions or problems she is having throughout her day, but that you will no longer see her frustrations as an excuse to act inappropriately. Explain to her that you will be willing to scratch her from classes, leave the show grounds, or interrupt her publicly. If she is as accomplished a child as you have described, she will have the emotional means to pull the punch.

Stick to your guns.

Many parents have difficulty knowing how much of their kid's bullish behavior or attitudes to tolerate before drawing a line. It's understandable; our culture teaches us that "kids are kids" and "teens will be teens." In our efforts to raise high-achieving, creative, and independent children, we have erred toward overgratifying them, and never more than now do they need us to hold them accountable for their choices and demonstrate a strong measure of faith in their ability to channel their desires and needs through the faculties of sensitivity, benevolence, and civility. Let your daughter know, Margaret, that you and your husband are willing to be very inconvenienced in order to help her become the kind of human being you will have been proud to raise.

NO TEAM, NO STEAM

Our adult lives are filled with extraordinary demands on our time and attention. Thus it's with great anticipation that many of us approach our riding lessons. The better part of an hour spent focused on . . . me? Not since my fourth-grade clarinet lessons have I enjoyed such fixed regard from an expert.

John, my husband, once told me how much he liked the individualized instruction this sport offers. He contrasted it with the years he spent playing football in high school, where coaching was hollered out to the group, each member to make his own sense out of it, alone in a crowd. Now, almost amazed, he reports after lessons, "Peter watches me the whole time! And the things he says are specific to me. It's the greatest."

So it is for many, much of the time.

But not always, and not for everybody. Oh, everything's all right as long as you're both whistling the same tunes, *but what if you're not?*

Clients tell me: "*My trainer has bigger goals for my riding than I will ever entertain. How can I tell her that her ideas don't mesh with mine without offending?*"

Let's fiddle first with goal-setting. Later we'll tackle diplomacy.

With eminent patience, history and common sense keep reminding us that setting riding goals must be a mutual process between rider and trainer. A trainer who's pulling a reluctant rider along on a program that the rider doesn't like will feel just the way she does riding the balky horse who won't go forward: The trainer inevitably winds up doing too much work—and resenting the whole darn thing. And the rider, on her end, doesn't like being sold up to the next level any more than does a prospective car buyer. For better or worse, the rider wants what she wants; fair enough—after all, she's the customer.

Nonetheless, as the rider, you do need to take responsibility for figuring out what it is you want from your sport and trainer, and discussing it with her or him when you first arrange for lessons. If your focus changes (you *can* change your mind, and goal-setting is always more of an evolving process than a static decision), or if you sense that your trainer's focus is changing, you discuss anew. This way, you never leave her or him in the dark as to how you feel about what the two of you are doing.

If you guys don't see eye to eye, explain to your trainer why you don't feel her ideas about goals are right for you. *She doesn't need to agree with you;* she just needs to appreciate and respect your point of view. Help her understand why the goals you've selected meet your needs better by understanding your own reasons well yourself. Your trainer might easily think your reluctance to do more than a few little shows a year is because of the added expense or time commitments. Who wouldn't? Seems logical. You yourself might even believe those are the reasons—until, on second thought, you discover that the real reason is you don't like being away from home overnight, or being too far away from your kids.

The more honest you can be with others, the easier it is for them to support you in the choices you make in life. So if you are frightened of the high fences in the next division up, say so. If you prefer winning prizes in smaller shows to gaining experience in larger ones, say so. If you don't want to step up your goals and have to leave behind your more limited horse, whom you love, say so.

As for not offending . . . no guarantees there. Some people will always be better (or worse) than others at hearing things that are at odds with what they believe to be right or true.

However, some people are also better (or worse) at telling others such things without making the person defensive. Your stating of differing goals needn't come off as a criticism of your trainer, or as a strident reassertion of control over your riding. Think collaboration instead of right or wrong. And be open to your trainer's thoughts about what else you could be doing with your riding, instead of dismissing them out of hand. If you bring up concerns in a timely, nonattacking, pleasant way, it becomes the other person's responsibility to respond in kind.

TIME TO LEAVE YOUR TRAINER?

Not all rider-trainer alliances wind up going the distance. Such partnerships begin with high hopes, ambitious plans, and lots of good will on both sides. But over time, differences of opinion and values and styles of relating can become increasingly noticeable to rider or trainer or both. And although these differences aren't necessarily problems in themselves (after all, we learn to love or work with or otherwise get along with a variety of people), occasionally they do create fault lines that crack open under the stress of training, performing, winning, and losing.

Here I'll give you some thoughts to guide you through the process of deciding whether or not to leave your trainer. You may discover alternatives to leaving that you hadn't seen before, or if you do wind up leaving, pick up ideas to make the relationship with your next trainer better.

GOOD REASONS FOR LEAVING

• **You repeatedly feel overfaced** by your trainer's exercises or expectations.

• **You feel undue pressure** being put on you to commit to a lesson or show program that is beyond your means or interest, even after you've clearly stated your wishes. Or maybe you've lost control of your horse's management or welfare in ways that you haven't authorized.

• **Your trainer frequently screams** to make a point, publicly humiliates you, or plays students off one another.

• **You and your trainer can't talk!** No one says you've got to be best buds, but you do need to be able to share your ideas and communicate what each of you needs/wants/doesn't like.

• **You strongly question your trainer's judgment** in relation to training, instructing, barn/horse management, or safety considerations.

• **You simply feel ready for more advanced training** than your current trainer can offer. Good instructors recognize when the time comes for you to move on, tell you so, and help with the transition.

BAD REASONS FOR LEAVING

- **Your trainer can't read your mind.**
- **Your trainer doesn't think you and your horse are as extraordinarily exceptional** as you believe.
- **Your trainer makes you think and function independently** of her at times.
- **Your trainer wants you to do more flatwork.**
- **Your trainer doesn't always treat you** as the most important person on the planet.

THINGS TO TRY BEFORE LEAVING

- **First, reflect honestly on your contribution to the mess**—rarely is any unsatisfactory situation all the other person's fault. In what ways are you too demanding, unrealistic, combative, defensive, or whiney? There's no shame in having a difficult part to your personality; just don't make it everyone else's problem.
- **Talk with your trainer.** Tried that already? Try it again. Say, "I just want you to know that in spite of the difficulties we sometimes have, I really like your training and am hoping we can work it out."
- **Try clinics with other trainers to gain perspective.** Maybe your trainer does know what she's talking about. Maybe you've overestimated your ability, or your horse's.

TIME TO GO?

If you're at the point where you're spending so much time either worrying about, trying to fix, or not enjoying your program that you can't focus on your riding, you're probably wise to consider a change.

UNINVITED ADVICE

Janet, a friend who boards in the same barn I do is distraught. A new boarder in our barn told my friend that the reason she was having a problem with her horse is that the horse most likely is sore and needs a chiropractor. This new boarder followed my friend around the barn for a half-hour, mentioning repeatedly that a chiropractor would be visiting the barn later that month and could see the horse.

By the time this person left, my friend was practically in tears, overwhelmed by all the lecturing and now worried that she wasn't properly caring for her horse's health needs. When she told the do-gooder that she had limited funds and had to be careful how she chose to spend them, she got a pep talk about how "our horses are worth it." Of course they're worth it—but not all of us are overflowing with money to indulge them in such luxuries! How can we deal with such lectures without appearing rude to them or uncaring about our horses? Yours truly, Peer Pressure

TOO MANY COOKS?

Used to be there were only one or two people to consult when you had a question about your horse—your trainer and your vet. Now there are gobs of horse health-care professionals: massage therapists, acupuncturists, chiropractors, and herbalists, among others. It's hard enough to sort through all these resources yourself and decide whom you want on your team. It's even harder when you have Ann and David and Joe and Mrs. Smith all telling you what *they* think you should do and which expert you should see.

On the other hand, PP, access to different (informed) opinions and points of view can be valuable. These days the line between mainstream and alternative veterinary treatments is a gray one; interventions that not so long ago raised eyebrows and evoked knowing smirks now make the standard program list in many barns. So we don't want to get stuck just following "the way we've always done it."

Most do-gooders offering advice mean well and have only the horse's best interests in mind. Some, though, can get pretty insistent, even self-righteous, making you feel like a lousy owner if you don't heed their wisdom. How to reply, PP, depends upon how you choose to balance exposure to these new perspectives and maintaining your autonomy and privacy about your horse's veterinary management.

WAYS TO RESPOND

I think a good first step would be to settle in with a veterinarian whose horse-care philosophy you share. Then make it a point to learn as much as possible (read, read, read, go to seminars, ask, pick brains, read some more) so you have some basis from which to judge other opinions, prospective treatments, and results.

When faced with suggestions that don't seem useful, you can say, "Thanks for your input. I'll have to see." This is an easy, pleasant way to let the suggester know he or she's been heard. In most cases, that's enough to persuade an "advisor" to move down the barn aisle and proselytize someone else. "I appreciate your input, but I think I'm going to stick with the program I have for now" is another option. This sends a polite but gentle "cease and desist" message to the do-gooder; all but the boorish will take the hint.

For those guys to whom you may need to say something a bit more emphatic, try "Look, I know you're trying to be helpful, but I'm afraid I'm not yet on board with those kinds of treatments. Maybe later on. Thanks, though." Or, if limited finances are a factor, you can say, "Thanks for your help, but my horse budget is limited for now. So I try to take care of as much as I can with more basic kinds of treatments." If the do-gooder retorts that the recommended treatment is "necessary," explain that one person's staple is another's luxury, and that you're doing the best you can.

Indeed, some things that were considered luxuries years ago are thought of as basic care in some barns today. But that doesn't mean you need to justify your choices to anyone but your vet, your trainer (*if* he or she is involved in your horse's program), and—most important—yourself and your horse.

FRIEND JEALOUS OF YOUR RIDING?

Irene writes: *I learned to ride in my twenties but had not ridden in some years. Recently, a dear friend and I decided to start riding again; we found a wonderful teacher and began taking weekly lessons.*

I advanced quickly and now enjoy riding around the countryside with friends and neighbors, riding horses belonging to them. My friend, however, advanced more slowly; she is still working in the safety of the ring on a gentle and reliable horse.

Now a problem has arisen: My friend has become jealous of me, and especially of my being invited to ride out with these folks. I don't have my own horse, so I welcome opportunities to ride other horses and go with people who know the trails in our area, but I know my doing so is painful for my friend.

My trainer tells me I need to go on with my riding and assures me my friend will advance at her own pace, but I worry that the situation is going to mar our friendship. Can you help?

When such issues arise between friends, tiptoeing around them can be tempting—but only makes matters worse. First of all, it creates a silent distance between the two of you: Each knows that something is wrong, but neither is saying anything about it. Second, because you're not talking about it, you give yourselves no opportunity to solve the problem. I promise you, these things don't go away. They settle in and, like bad houseguests, take over. And, third, you guys send a terrible message to each other that you don't believe your friendship is hardy enough to manage a difficult problem together.

Irene, I think the best and most honest thing to do in your situation is to go straight to your friend and tell her exactly what you just told me. The problem concerns the two of you, so there's no reason you need to solve it alone. Let your friend help with the solution.

Start by saying something like, "I so much enjoy our riding together, but I've noticed a problem and am worried that it will affect our friendship. I don't want that to happen. I'm aware that our riding programs are changing, and that more and more I'm going out to ride with others while you stay back. We're not riding together as much as we were, and I feel bad about that. Do you?"

If your friend responds by saying, "Hey, let's not sweat it. Go ahead, have a ball, and I'll catch up," you'll know that you can ride on without worrying about how she's faring. Even if she says, "I miss riding together, and sometimes I worry you'll go off with your buddies and forget about me completely," you guys are still in good shape because of the candor and forthrightness in your relationship. Having problems isn't what hurts a relationship; what does the damage is not having the communication skills and faith in one another to deal with those problems. If your friend is worried about getting left in the dust, let her know that you intend to include her everywhere you can, and that your unmounted time together will likely be unchanged.

If, however, she says, "Do what you have to, Irene . . ."—well, then, you guys are in deep doo-doo. You might try saying, "Hearing you speak like that makes me sad, as if you resent me for going on. I can't imagine you'd expect me to pass on some of these rides. Let's come up with a better solution—our friendship shouldn't depend on our riding programs."

And it shouldn't. And can't. You'd be miserable if you held yourself back to keep the peace, and the friendship would die a slow, miserable death anyway. Consider instead all the things you can still do together, no matter what your respective riding levels are—grooming, shopping for tack, spectating, riding together in the ring a bit before you go out with other riders. How about your friend going with you for short walks around the property where your barn is?

You're a good friend to have taken the initiative on this. Losing a friendship through passive silence is sad. Keep a dialogue going and try your best to keep friendship alive—it's too important.

FRIEND AND FOE

A dressage rider who shows regularly writes in, asking how she can stay both competitive and friendly with a good buddy who rides in the same classes as she does. Terri says that . . . *so far things are fine. But as we move up, I'm afraid we'll run into problems. For myself, I have to psych myself up a bit to be competitive, and that's pretty hard if you're feeling guilty about beating your best friend. . . .*

I get asked this question so much that I probably didn't even have to disguise Terri's name (although I did). Yet competing against people we care about isn't something that happens for the first time at a horse show. We've competed with siblings for our parents' attention, with classmates for our teachers' recognition, and with friends for the popular vote. We compete now, still—with coworkers for a supervisor's regard, perhaps with family members for the best laughs at the Thanksgiving table. Most of the time it's not obvious. Most of the time it's benign.

Practice doesn't always make perfect, though, and not everyone is an expert at balancing competitiveness with devotion to loved ones and friends. Some people become hell-bent on winning, even at the cost of their relationships, while others quash all competitive instincts in unnecessary and false deference to their friends.

But balance isn't so hard to achieve *if you learn to trust both your genuine interest in your friendships and your competitive side.*

Many athletes worry that it's wrong to "beat" friends. That's an issue especially for many of the female riders I talk with or hear from. Taught from an early age to "be nice," taught early on that "good girls" are not aggressive, they learn to mute their competitive urges. *How can I want to win,* wonders the young girl, *and be a nice kid, too?*

Well, there are ways—because it's never been true that good girls don't get tough. They just don't get nasty. So here are some tips, Terri, on helping you find that balance.

• **Wanting yourself to do well and wanting your friends to do well at shows are not mutually exclusive desires; both can be true.** It's only that you want to do, well, a little better than your friend does—not because you're mean, but because you are a normal competitor. If you weren't, you wouldn't be at a horse show.

• **Placing better than your friend "beats" her in one sense of the word but not in another.** You're no more decimating her than you decimate your cousin or your grandma in a heated game of Monopoly.

• **And even if you are more competitive than most, so be it.** You are who you are. If you don't like it, you *can* change it—but in the meantime, within you there exists a large measure of safety against your becoming a cannibal. It is your (our) human ability to think or feel something but not allow yourself to act on it. So as long as you know you're not going to lock your friend in the portapotty as her class is being called, or do something similarly dastardly, you're OK. You deal with feelings you don't like in yourself by deciding ahead of time how you want to act and committing to that in spite of how you may actually feel. If you want to be a dignified sportsperson, consider what such a person would say and do in competitions—and then say and do just that. Feelings you can't always help; actions you can.

• **At the same time, Terri, be alert to when your feelings of wanting to win might be compromising your friendship.** If you begin to get overly preoccupied with matters of justice, fairness, and right and wrong at the expense of enjoying your friend's company, or if you find yourself resenting her success and getting picky about her performance, then reflect on your balance of competitiveness and true-blueness.

But I'll tell you, there's nothing about your letter to suggest you are out of balance. You seem like an insightful individual who wants to be both a good rider *and* a good friend. I believe the answer lies in *allowing yourself to do both well*—in being the best competitor you can be and the best friend you can be. Holding back on either your riding or the relationship makes a sham of both.

SURVIVING A FAMILY
RIDING BUSINESS

Dear Janet: I help run a hunter/jumper barn that's been in my family for decades. Over the past two years I have gradually been taking over the teaching responsibilities from my mom, who's been instructing boarders and other riders ever since she started a lesson program almost twenty years ago. She still teaches the people who go to the bigger shows, but I've been teaching the beginner and intermediate riders, as well as some of the more advanced kids and adults when my mom is away at shows. I'm also taking business courses at a local college so I can one day become more involved in the operation of the farm.

The problem is that my mom wants me to do everything exactly the same way that she does. Although I greatly respect her knowledge and teaching skills, I also have my own style and ideas, and some of my ideas work pretty well with certain students whom she's had trouble reaching.

We're starting to argue, which is really no fun when we both work at the same place all day long and live at the same place at night. I don't want to be disrespectful, but I don't want to feel so stuck having to copy her.

Have you ever heard of this kind of thing before? Do you have any ideas for me? —Pat

Yes, I have ideas for you, Pat. Actually, some psychological consultants do nothing but help families who run businesses together. Members of such families typically do a lot of wrestling over who makes the big decisions, whether to institute new methods or stick with the tried and true, and when and how to transfer power to the next generation. You're far from alone in your dilemma.

Here are a couple of points worth considering.

• **Don't think that the tension between you and your mom means you two have an unusual or insurmountable problem.** What you describe is a normal and predictable part of both running a family business and becoming an adult. Heightened conflict between the two of you probably would have shown up anyway, even if you hadn't started working at the farm. It's a necessary pathway for your movement into adulthood and for your mother's endorsement of your independence and autonomy. The riding business simply provides an easy backdrop for this developmental transition.

• **Expend your biggest effort in maintaining an open dialogue with your mom about all these matters.** Tell her directly and clearly that you respect her training ideas and business savvy, but that at the same time you're trying to define your own training and management style in response to your expanded responsibilities. Discuss with your mom which areas of the business she thinks are essential to be kept as is, and in which she would be more accepting of change.

• **It's very important that your mom not feel everything she's worked so hard to build is at risk** of being disassembled as you assume more and more responsibility for the farm's operations. She may believe this threat is far greater than is actually the case; it is apparent that you deeply respect her expertise. To help her feel safer viewing you more as a partner and less as an assistant, find opportunities to emphasize aspects of her program that you value highly. Another thing that might help is to assure her that you will try—even in the heat of battle—to recognize when her way really is the better way.

• **Whenever conversations become tense, remind each other that you two really want the same things:** a sound operation, happy customers. Remind yourself, too, that being independent does not mean you're being a traitor. (Do be aware, though, that if your ideas begin to differ markedly from those of your mom, you may have to consider how well you can do business in her barn—it is *her* barn.)

Keep coming back to the table for more discussion, even if that discussion has to happen at another time or on another day. Don't avoid talking about the problem just because doing so is awkward, hoping it will ease up. It won't. Then you'll really dread returning to the house in the evening—and there are only so many nighttime barn checks you can go out to do!

SPEAKING OF AGGRESSION

Recently a reader asked how to manage being both friendly and competitive with a dressage pal of hers. Wanting to do well and wanting your friends to do well are not mutually exclusive, I said. What really matters is not how competitive someone feels inside, but how she responds to and acts on those feelings. Sportsmanship is sportsmanship, apart from whatever zealousness you feel in your heart.

I added that riders striving to be competitive must eventually do something that is often difficult: get comfortable with their aggressiveness and then weave it into their riding technique and judgment. Because without some aggressiveness in the mix, riders ride too carefully—wishing instead of intending, considering instead of committing. "I tried to make him go to the left, but he didn't want to" is one rider's experience while "You're going to the left, bucko. Now, by the way" is another's. No screaming, no jerking, no whips, no big drama. Just "it's going to happen." Period.

The difficulty? People back off their aggressive side for any number of reasons. Some, due to upbringing or values, have a very low tolerance for any display of aggression, even when it's for a good cause, as in speaking out for safer foods and better schools, or riding a horse forward through a combination. They mistake it for something that is always and by definition mean or nasty or uncivilized. Others shy away because they worry (or know) that aggression will spin out of control on them, making them harsh, unsympathetic, abusive. But abuse and its cousins are examples of aggression gone awry, divorced from reason and self-control. Shunning aggression outright is akin to throwing the baby out with the bath water.

There are yet other reasons that riders back off the gas pedal. Today, after a week out of town, I was schooling my horse on the flat. I was gently and patiently "reintroducing" him to forwardness, balance, straightness, and rhythm; he was lugging along. And suddenly I thought, what is this "reintroducing"? We've been doing this for more than a year. He doesn't need "re" anything. He needs a poke in the belly and a tug on his left side and a growl. So I did these things. His response? A work ethic. I'd needed to ride him more aggressively, not play the warm fuzzy.

Later on I realized that, for me, too, riding aggressively means having to work my way mentally through a bit of a wall. But my wall is a different one. When I ride too aggressively, I don't feel immoral or get abusive—I get reckless. Years ago, when I put the pedal to the metal on course, I'd end up making it happen, but I was scary to watch sometimes. I don't do that now, mainly because I'm a better rider. But I wonder if my ride is more moderate not only because I've refined my skills, but also because I've become a less aggressive rider. I often question if I'd be a bolder rider, a less conservative rider—I hate to say it, but a better rider still— if I were not one of two heads of a family with three young children.

I'm not saying my wall of safety and restraint is rational or correct, but it is what I have to wrestle with. And in the end, I do worry about giving Agassi too aggressive a ride and making the kinds of rash decisions in timing and striding that were marginally survivable a few years back but would be downright dangerous now, in the bigger jumper divisions. I don't want to go back there, yet I also know that I need to tap into some of that daring or I'll fizzle my way through courses.

But I think I've figured out something else, too; that when we become uncomfortable tapping into our aggressiveness, it's often because we're confusing attitude with action. Riding aggressively, like being competitive, has much more to do with how you are feeling inside than with what you are doing outside. You ride differently when you ride aggressively; that's the whole point. But it's a subtle difference in your application of aids, in the certainty of your decisions, and in that measure of confidence you radiate into your horse that makes him go better. Like so much else in life, it's all about balance.

UNWILLING WITNESS

Young Janey sends in a letter about her friend—the kind of letter that no one ever wants to have to write: *I strongly believe that my friend is neglecting her horse. When I first met Amie, she was taking excellent care of Blue. Over the past year, though, that care has gone from spending hours with him to just getting the job done. Now Blue is laid up with swollen joints from being stuck in a dirty stall. His salt block is moldy, and his water is green. A friend of mine who works for the humane society says there isn't enough proof to charge Amie. What should I do?*

Different problems keep people from taking proper care of their animals, but those problems don't mean beans to the animal who's stuck in a stall or field somewhere, cold or hungry or hurt. Here are some things to try, Janey, and let's hope one of them reaches through to your friend. She had it in her once to take good care of Blue, and that's a good sign.

• **Start by talking directly with Amie in a supportive and non-critical way.** Let her know you're not trying to make her feel bad or embarrassed, just trying to refocus her attention. You still run a pretty high risk of getting the cool shoulder, though; people don't like to be told their animals are unhappy. They get defensive ("I know how to take care of my own horse, thank you") or mad ("Why don't you worry about your own horse if you want to be so critical?!") or sullen and withdrawn. If this happens, calmly tell her what you've noticed, and offer to help for a while. If Amie tells you to lay off, let her know that you're sorry she is offended but you're also worried enough to share your observations with an adult on the property.

• **If it's your lucky day (and Blue's), Amie will be surprised at your comments and sincerely ask what you mean.** The door then opens for you to tell her (gently) or show her (kindly). There's always the possibility your friend is acting out of ignorance or misinformation.

• **If you don't feel you can talk to Amie directly, consider writing her a letter.** Sign your name, though! Invisible enemies are the worst kind. You could always do the old Ann Landers thing, too, and leave a copy of this column out for her to see (just add your name).

• **Why, by the way, are you wrestling with this on your own?** Where's the trainer—or, if it's a private barn, the owner? Can you join forces with another boarder? Would your parents be willing to speak to Amie's parents?

• **Call your local SPCA or large-animal protection organization and ask officials there** (not your friend, who may not have the relevant experience) for advice. Is there something they advise you not to do, to avoid making the situation worse? People can react strangely to what they think is meddling; they may remove the animal to a more isolated location, act aggressively toward concerned parties, or even (in extreme cases) take their frustrations out on the animal. Amie sounds young and naive and an unlikely candidate for the above, but it makes sense to have solid guidance. The most important thing is to try to communicate to Amie that you're coming at this as her friend, and as a friend of animals.

Sadly, Janey, you could do all of this and still get nowhere with helping Blue. Then it becomes important for you to manage the despair and sense of helplessness that may follow. Otherwise, hearts get heavy and hard, and people learn to turn away from those whose blank looks or withered bodies silently call for help. There may be one in another bunch that you can save.

Letting yourself care and feel as you do is a very brave thing, and it involves an emotional risk. But it's rewarded many times over by the relief of those you help, and by the richer texture of your own emotional life.

Do just as you're doing, Janey, and then some. This is a case that neither begins nor ends with Blue, but for Blue it's everything in his world. Give it your best.

MAKING SPORTSMANSHIP MATTER

Dear Janet: I run a summer riding camp, and I regularly bring in vets, farriers, and other clinicians to expose the kids to different aspects of horsemanship. The one topic I can't seem to tackle is sportsmanship. Any time I've tried, the whole thing comes off as a lecture; before I know it, the kids are rolling their eyes. Even I get bored hearing myself! Any ideas for enlivening the subject? —Maria

Hats off to you, Maria, for addressing this topic. It gets a lot more lip service than playing time, but any sport churning out as many kid competitors as riding ought to include the subject in its curriculum. The problem—as you know! —is making an impact on young minds that really only want to know when their next ride is. Here are a few ideas:

• **Inspire, don't preach.** Some things in life are better exemplified than taught, and sportsmanship is definitely one of them. The ideas of honor, teamwork, graciousness in victory or defeat, and so on get absorbed best when they are living, breathing parts of a barn and its operations. Find ways to integrate them into everything kids do—horse care, barn management, common manners—and not just competing.

Ask your campers which riders or national sports heroes demonstrate sportsmanship the best—or the worst. Ask provocative questions: What if Tonya Harding were their sister? Their riding instructor? Do they think Dennis Rodman is a good sport or not? If they were writing a book called *The Seven Daughters of Mrs. Torts Really Are the Very Worst Sports*, what would the characters be like? Have them act it out in a skit. Create problem scenarios for them to solve in small groups (e.g., "You know something about how a course rides that your barn mate doesn't. Do you share the info?"). Play! You can make the topic relevant without making your riders think they've enrolled in a Modern Ethics course.

• **Clarify "healthy" competitiveness.** Help your young riders distinguish between being hungry to win and being nasty. Some think there's no such thing as a nice winner. They're wrong. "Good sport" competitors target their aggressiveness toward the course or test, not toward fellow riders. But don't get Pollyanna-ish and dismiss your kids' desires to get to the winner's circle, or your talks won't sound genuine.

If you have kids whose parents regularly model unsportsmanlike behavior, you'll probably have to speak with the grownups yourself. Such parents are likely too intimidating for a child to talk to about "toning it down." Finding the words might be hard, but any young rider in your charge whose parent acts inappropriately deserves your assistance. And don't be afraid of losing a client; your speaking up is part of being a professional, operating your business in ways that match your values.

• **Tell 'em they're doing it right!** To Sandy, who tried her hardest at the camp horse show with no ribbons to show for it, say, "You were a great sport! I know you were disappointed, but you kept a smile on your face from morning to night. It was a pleasure spending the day with you." . . . To Eric, learning to ride in a crowded ring: "You just showed the best manners of any pony rider I've ever seen! I'm proud to have you in my barn."

• **And for those who don't get it . . .** Got two kids who just won't stop sneering at each other? Speak with them together privately. Tell them that you've noticed their problem and that they need to take care of it. Don't let yourself be used as a sounding board for complaints and whining, but do offer assistance if they seem genuinely to want to work things out.

When they find out their fussing has become obvious to others, they might become self-conscious enough to square up their accounts and move on. If they don't, send them out for a day to volunteer together at your local SPCA or large-animal protection society. And if they still can't get the job done, then have them groom for each other—exclusively—until they do.

TRAINING TEENAGERS!

Instructor Kim writes in: *Some of my teenage riders have become diffi-cult for me to deal with during lessons. They act like know-it-alls, and they don't seem to respect my instruction as much as before. What's hap-pened, and what can I do about it?*

Several explanations are possible, Kim, but I'll mention three likely factors.

• **We're Not in Kansas Any More.** Teaching teens is different from teaching kids. The latter are a pretty straightforward lot, posing teaching dilemmas of another sort: shorter attention spans, needing complex ideas simplified. But as kids get to be thirteen and fourteen, their bodies and minds start changing on them—and they begin, unavoidably, to wrestle with various psychological conflicts. For instance, they want independ-ence but are afraid of it. They don't like having to rely on adults, but at the same time they find comfort in adult guidance.

These conflicts aren't particular about settings—kitchens, class-rooms, soccer fields all see their share. So it's not surprising that they show up in the riding ring, too. Throughout the day, your teens may var-iously be moody, clingy, or strong-willed. Some of these behaviors and attitudes you will find acceptable; others you won't.

How to deal with the unacceptable?

1. Speak with the student individually: "Look, I understand that being fifteen is no picnic, but the sarcasm in your responses has got to stop. Tuck it in or take a pass on your lesson for today."

2. Speak to a lesson group: "You guys have gotten wild and woolly with your know-it-all attitudes. You need to know that I will ask you to leave the ring if it happens again."

3. Speak to a teen with her family.

4. Curtail privileges around the barn (schooling horses, showing).

• **"I Went into This Business to Be Around Horses, Not to Manage People!"** Horse professionals generally *do* choose their careers so they can spend more time with horses. As they get established, though, they find themselves having to deal with things other than horses—money, customers, staffing, et cetera. Some they may be good at; some not.

If, for instance, Kim, you're not as good at setting limits as you are at teaching, your operation—and your riders' attitudes—might have become too casual. Because another trademark of adolescence is repeatedly testing the limits set by adults, your students may sense your preference for being "one of the guys" over being "the boss" and use that as an opportunity to take advantage of you. One way they can do this is by goofing on the things they're "told" to do—even if they really believe in them. It's their way of telling you that they're not taking you seriously enough—and a cue to you that you need to change how you are managing your role around the barn.

A good way to learn to do this is by watching other trainers whose "people skills" you respect and see how they manage to be friendly with their kids yet keep their professionalism. Observe how they interact in lessons and enforce barn rules. Pay special attention to what they say, so you can borrow effective expressions and use them at home.

• **Is Your Lesson Program "Ho-hum" or "Oh, Wow!"?** Your teens might be acting up because they're bored. Keep your instruction fresh by introducing new exercises, games on horseback, "guest" instructors (swap teaching responsibilities with another trainer for a day!). Establish individual programs and get feedback regularly, so you can pick up on areas of discontent early—before it seeps out and affects the mood of the whole group. Kids love to gripe in groups; it doesn't even have to be their gripe—anybody's will do!

Teaching teenagers has its occupational hazards, Kim. But don't let it discourage you. On the whole, teens love to learn new things—and love their horses. They're a lively, appealing group. Try to bear with some of their clowning while you learn better ways to manage their inappropriate behavior.

Whatever you do, though, don't take it too personally. Remember that we once tortured the adults around us in very much these same ways!

[CHAPTER 5]

Balancing Riding with Everything (And Everyone) Else in Your Life

'I'M A WORKAHOLIC...'

So begins a letter from a reader *"who feels guilty about spending time and money riding."* This old malady, as rampant now among women as it has long been among men, claims another victim with nasty bouts of anxiety, inner conflict, and undeserved self-reproach. The owner of a small business finally enough in the black to allow a return to riding, Renee has had trouble justifying the time riding entails. Recovering from injury and in need of a break from her work and physical-therapy schedule, she wants to take up her friend's offer of a loaner horse, *"but the stable is an hour away and I'm feeling guilty about taking that much time for recreation. My morale would certainly benefit from the riding, but how can I manage the guilt?"*

The illusion that we could ever get all our work done has always been a cruel temptress. Assured that we will finally feel at ease, finally be worry-free, finally feel deserving of the fruits our labors have borne, we march along in dogged pursuit of the crossed-off list of errands, the last returned call, the clear desk. Ahhh, we whisper, it's right around the corner, just a little more now, surely soon I'll be done. But we are scammed once again. Isn't there always another assignment, a new call, more mail?

Renee, here are some ideas for you, along with some questions to ponder:

• **You care for your new business six days a week plus.** You don't say the business needs *you*, specifically, to be present each of those hours; you say you feel bad leaving it. If the business *can* run well in your absence for periods of time, go. How? You go by fighting the impulse to stay, and riding *in spite of the guilt* until you reach a place mentally that doesn't involve feeling guilty when you ride. People are always waiting until they feel differently to go ahead and change. That's a mistake. Act first, and how you feel will change afterward. You are correct in asking how to *manage* the guilt, rather than asking how to (magically) rid yourself of it. The guilt will go away once you begin to think differently about your work, your riding, and yourself. Read on for how to do that. And if your business can't run well without you there, get a "sitter" who knows it well and will effectively cover for you. You nurtured a business to financial solvency. Now do something nice for yourself.

• **Speaking of doing something nice for yourself, I imagine that this happens too rarely, lasts too briefly;** any good workaholic worth her salt shortchanges herself this way. Consider using a personal ditty or slogan to help push yourself over that hump toward pleasure and your riding. Examples include terms such as *perspective* or *balance*, or phrases like *balance in life leads to less inner strife, a horse on course means no remorse, all work and no play will make me very dull today,* and so on. The sillier, the better.

• **Create a "material" slogan, or "symbol,"** to help urge you out of the workplace and up to that barn. For instance, let's say that during one very special trail ride you were moved by the early-morning sighting of several deer and their fawns. You appreciated deeply then why riding is such an important part of your life. So you go to a store and look for a little ceramic or brass deer, small enough to fit into your purse or pocket, that you carry around with you. And whenever you even *begin* to have doubts that riding is a valid and valuable piece of your pie, you take out your figurine, hold it, talk to it, whatever, and let it tell you what you need to remember.

• **One final point.** You're very good at adhering to the time-demanding rehab instructions of your medical doctors for your physical pain. Yet you write that you *"feel pressured and worn out"* and *"badly need time off."* Why should your emotional needs carry less importance? Let the authority of your own self weigh as influentially as that of your doctor.

Besides, with all that effort at work going out, something's got to come in. Nothing runs without fuel. Recreation isn't just getting away from it all; dictionaries tell us its purpose is to refresh ourselves, to impart new life to our minds and bodies. That sounds important enough to me. Go ride.

DON'T RUN, DON'T HIDE

Dr. Edgette, you have written time and again about the difficulties of learning to ride as an adult. One problem is the inability to empty all our thoughts from our stressful days and then ride. Of late, I haven't been able to keep separate these two parts of my life.

I work a full-time job whose future has now become uncertain. My husband will be leaving his job due to a career-ending illness, and we will be forced to move. Need I add that we have two kids in college? . . .

The root of my stress is that I'm trying desperately to hold on to the horse I've had for eleven years, not to mention the lessons and hunter paces that have been goals of mine for so long. I'm forty-seven and my horse is nineteen—we don't have forever. . . .

How do I continue riding if I can't stay focused? For weeks now I've been making mistakes in my lessons and not knowing why. I go off course, go blank. . . . Can you help me focus again while all of this is going on? Should I put my riding on the back burner for a while? Please help. —Jeri

Jeri, you're working too hard!—too hard at keeping stress from affecting your riding. Figure that it already has, and that there are better ways to beat this. After all, you really can't separate "you" the rider from "you" the person; that's why so many of us ride horses the same way we live life—boldly or cautiously, "perfectly" or comfortably, with humor and perspective or without. We are who we are.

Worry if you must, and don't try to fight the thoughts. Let them come and go during your day; stay fluid and dynamic in your mind. Don't hang onto any one thought, or debate them, or try to hide from them. Listen casually to them, and then go about your business. The point here, as in the management of anxiety, is not to force psychological phenomena one way or another, but rather to learn to do what you need or want to do in spite of them.

What eventually happens, ironically, is that once you take the fight out of it, worrying can quietly move into the background. Suddenly and subtly, everything changes.

Here are some other points to keep in mind during this stressful period:

• **Ride, Jeri.** Don't stop just because it doesn't feel the same as before or doesn't go as smoothly. Give yourself room to have periods when your riding is awkward or unfamiliar or just plain unlikable. I know it's not your preferred ride, but it's an honest ride for you right now. Put a hold on your lessons or paces if you want, but don't stay away from the barn. Putting your riding on the back burner because it feels different allows your need for it to be "just right" to take you away from your horse.

• **Talk to your husband about your experience of this time of crisis in your lives.** Tell him what frightens you, worries you, reassures you. Ask him what he worries about. Tell him you're scared of losing your horse and why that is so important to you. Be sensitive to how he might hear that while he struggles with a career-ending illness. The idea is not to compare losses, but to go through the experience as supportively and intimately as possible.

• **Get proactive and make plans for all contingencies.** If, eventually, you will need to slash expenses, line up a friend who would be able to keep your horse for you for nominal expense. Think about services you could barter for—maybe shoeing, training, or veterinary services? Find backup arrangements in case things fall through.

Making contingency plans for the worst won't (as people sometimes secretly fear) make the bad thing any more likely to happen, but it will make whatever happens easier to deal with if things don't go your way. Moreover, it will give you a feeling of control about the future and thus some peace of mind as you and your husband navigate through these difficult circumstances. It might even make some of the worries go away.

MORE BABIES OR MORE HORSES?

Dear Janet: I recently completed vet school and am looking forward to having time again to ride. But with a one-year-old daughter, I'm still scrambling to ride two or (if I'm lucky) three times a week. I know you have three young kids and a dedication to your riding and your career, so I was wondering if you have advice for trying to balance it all. My dilemma is that I'd always wanted two children, but now I'm just starting to enjoy my free(er) time. My horse is going well. I've got a great trainer. And I don't know if I want to give that all up again to have another baby. It seems so selfish, but I like my life as it is, and I really love riding, and I want to have more time to ride. On the other hand, will having one more baby interfere that much more? Is it just a temporary inconvenience for a lifelong joy? —Eve

Eve, there are few decisions more personal than whether or not to have more children, but I'll share some thoughts to help you (and presumably your partner) sort through the process of deciding.

One baby is a piece of cake. She may not always sleep when you want her to, but she pretty much goes where you go. Life stays relatively quiet. And you still have a hand free to fish for your wallet, your keys, the butter in the fridge. Or, if you prefer, for boot pulls, a hoof pick, horse treats.

Two babies, or a baby and a toddler, is a whole different enchilada. One wakes up when the other goes to sleep. You have no hands free.

A recent study by family-life researchers noted that couples with one child usually manage to fit that child comfortably into their routine, more or less. Couples with two or more children wind up with dramatically changed family routines.

Not to mention dramatically changed noise and activity levels. John and I are always stunned by how quiet and still the house seems if we have only one of our three home. Everything seems—well, just so easy. Add two more to the mix and, even in the best of times, I feel as if I'm in a unending game of three-card monte.

Eve, I know you worry about being selfish if you stop after one child, but "selfish" can be another word for foresight. You know what your needs are, and the needs of the rest of your family. If, in your assessment, you come away saying, "I like my life as it is," to whom do you owe something else?

Some people will tell you that you owe your child a sibling. I disagree. You primarily owe your child love and safety and decisions that work for your family as you want to shape it—not necessarily a brother or sister. We all manage to make do with what we have, or we have the option to find it elsewhere in our lives.

On the other hand, if you want more in your life—another child, more riding—you may have to be willing to pay a price. It may not be too steep if you have enough resources and energy and desire, but there will likely be other things you give up. Or you may find it *is* too steep, in which case either you'll march on anyway, because you desperately want your children and your horses both, or you'll put your riding and other (relative) expendables on hold.

And you must not forget your partner, who inevitably pays the price with you. You need a way to make sure he doesn't feel lost in the mix, or taken for granted. In what ways can you reciprocally devote yourself to him, or to the dreams he wants to realize, as well as to your own?

Probably the most comforting thing I can tell you, Eve, is that it's not a decision you have to make today. There's always at least a little bit of time. Take that time and, together with your partner, plan to build a family that suits all of you. You may feel differently after you've had more time to enjoy your freedom from school, or when your daughter is a little older. Or you may not. Have confidence in your ability to make sound decisions on your and your family's behalf; I do.

ONE HALF OF A STORY

Dear Janet: It's 7:00 p.m. on a Sunday night, and I'm just getting back from a horse show. I've been gone since dawn, and I've spent so much money in entry fees, training fees, shipping fees, etc., that I can barely stand it— let alone the thought of coping with my surly husband, who is waiting for me at the door. Whatever can I say to him to avoid yet another cold war over the horse?—Marie

Looks like there already have been some border skirmishes. Don't worry, Marie. Feistier souls than you two have later wound up sitting together at the campfire.

Often, in these situations, the problem stems from one partner's feeling that the other's level of commitment to the sport seems greater than her commitment to the relationship. It's not a man or woman thing, but rather a couples thing, with matters of balance, accountability, and trust figuring most critically.

Here, Marie, I'll approach the question primarily from the point of view of the rider. In the next column, the non-riding spouse will get a turn.

I'll start with some of the more obvious ideas, then follow with considerations you may not have thought of. Sometimes, it turns out, we save our kindest, most courteous acts for strangers and leave our honeys to fend for themselves.

• **There's nothing like being included** in something to make you favorably disposed toward it. Have you invited your husband out to the barn with you, and to shows with you? I don't mean just "Wanna come?" but "I know you're not so into this, but I really like it when you come to my lessons. I like your company. Come and hang out with me, would you? We can be home by noon."

• **Have you helped your husband understand** the sport sufficiently that he can appreciate your love of it? It's not enough to say your horse is "running off with you down the lines" or is "heavy in the bridle again." Talk about the way it moves you when you nail the combinations. Describe to him your euphoria when your horse transforms into a gummy-bear under your nose. If he laughs and says, "Jeez, it's only riding, and he's only a horse!" laugh along with him and tell him that yeah, it must sound weird, but it really is that special. Don't get defensive. Instead, see it from his perspective and you'll realize how intoxicated we must at times sound talking about our riding. And if he continues to laugh or demean your riding, tell him that his doing so bothers you, and that if he can't be a fan of your riding, at least he can be a better sport about it.

• **Be honest and accurate** about the demands your riding places on you. If you think you'll be out past dinner, say so: "This show could run late, so go ahead and eat if I'm not back by 8:00; we'll have dessert together later. I'll keep you posted from the show as best I can." Don't say you'll be home by 6:00 because it sounds good to say it and there's a slight chance you could be back by then. Don't say the show will probably only run $50 or so for the day when you think it will probably run higher. If time or money is an issue, deal with it ahead of time, apart from the show itself, so the show doesn't become the spark that brings down the forest.

• **Appreciate how easy it can be** for spouses to feel jealous of something their partners love passionately. It's not necessarily your husband's fault that he looks so unhappy when you come home—he may be feeling way out of the loop in what is a very important part of your life.

• **Most important,** tell your husband that you don't want a cold war—before one starts. Don't assume he knows. When you actually say it, he'll realize you really mean it. Try to generate helpful ideas while staying emotionally connected to one another. Coming up with an immediate solution is less important than your both feeling that the two of you are approaching problems from the same side of the fence. It's when you draw enemy lines between you that things will stay hairy. You are not each other's enemy; the conflict is.

THE OTHER HALF OF THE STORY

In the last column, Marie asked for help in preventing the same ol' same ol' argument she and her husband have every time she arrives home after a long day away at a horse show. She didn't want a silent war, but she felt entitled to the riding that was bringing her so much pleasure. I offered some tips, but I also alluded to there being another way of looking at the situation than from her perspective.

That other way is through the eyes of the one at home, and you might be surprised at some of the things he (or she) would like to say if he knew the right words or found the right time. I hear those words in my office, and I want to pass them along to you.

• **"You know, I'm not out to cause trouble here.** I know your riding is important to you. It's just that I want to feel as if I'm important to you, too, and I don't. Or at least not as important to you as the horses seem."

Now here's a candid statement. But think about it. With all the pampering and enthusiasm and attention that go to the horse, your partner's feeling this way isn't all that "unexpectable." The solution isn't in doing less, but in having the other person in your life know that you would do as much for him. He may not want the curry-and-carrot routine, but there are ways to make him feel very important. Find some.

Other things I hear . . .

• **"Sometimes it's hard for me to see** something else give you more joy than I seem to do these days."

Well, how would *you* feel if you believed you couldn't hold a candle to the way your partner's pet makes him smile? If you think he thinks this, ask him: "This may sound funny, but do you ever worry that . . . ?"

And if he says yes? Don't panic. Appreciate his candor, for one thing. And appreciate the humor of the situation, and perhaps the need to add something to the relationship so that you laugh at least as much at home with your partner as you do at the barn.

• **"I wouldn't resent the horses if** I felt there was some room in our lives for me to devote myself to something that brought me such pleasure. But I worry that there are too few resources left. Or that if I did get involved in something, we'd never see each other. Sometimes I think the only way for me to spend any time with you is if I don't do anything else. So I don't."

You can't have all the goodies for yourself. Maybe your guy does need something of his own to balance out this consuming sport of yours. What unrealized dreams does he have, and how can you help him touch them? What are you willing to give up? Where are you willing to be flexible? *Even if he never calls on you to do it,* he'll appreciate that you would if he did.

This sport is truly extreme in its demands, and disagreements can arise without there ever having to be a "bad" guy. When there are chronic underlying tensions between a couple about the horses, it's very easy for any riding-related event to blow up into an argument. The kindling lies everywhere—in a charge on the credit card, in a late return from a lesson, in an injury. . . . And feeling war-weary, defensive, depressed, or angry, one or both in a couple can find themselves using the incident opportunistically as a means for trying, once again, to prove the other wrong or to "settle the score."

If this is what's happening in your home, you need instead to pull the punch, bite your tongue, and resist the urge to "win" the battle—because you are losing the war.

Tell your partner outright, at the first sign of trouble, that you want to find a way out of it, and expressly invite him (or her) to join you in finding it. Once you present yourself (yes, you go first) as willing to honor a genuine effort—no matter if it takes weeks or months—to keep your riding from coming between the two of you, then you have beautifully positioned yourselves to move beyond the problem.

HERE WE GO AGAIN

I just bought a new horse. I hadn't planned to do this. I wasn't even looking—*I really wasn't.* As with the two other horses I've bought in my
adult life, it just happened.

You see, I have ten-month-old twins and a four-year-old, all boys. My
husband and I make evenings together out of snatches of time between ten
and midnight, during which we also eat dinner, return calls, check e-mail,
pick up baby toys, and make sure we're not both scheduled to fly out of town
the next day. Oh, yeah, I almost forgot: Our townhouse is up for sale, and
one of these days *someone* will make *some* kind of an offer and we'll be
forced not only to pack up but to deal with the avalanching boxes and tee-
tering old furniture in our basement. I'm talking Project. Like I have time
for a horse right now?

And this isn't any horse. *He's* a project, too. I'd been riding him—a very
green sales horse in my trainer's barn—for a few months now, just to
rebuild my fitness and begin to get back in the game, but the big chestnut
kept looking better and better . . . until finally my trainer and I figured he
was my best shot at owning something that could jump a big fence and that
wouldn't keep me in debt for the rest of my life. (Heard this story before?)

Not that buying him isn't a stretch, mind you. But, hey, there's always
next year to add to those retirement funds, and there are still a few years
before we need to get *really* serious about those three college tuitions. And
then, of course, there's always plastic. . . .

And here I was just getting accustomed to life (for a little while) without a horse. I'd sold my last jumper in the fall and was just going to sit chilly
and save up my pennies. So much time now! So much less laundry! So much
more money around! I'd poke along through the mall with my stretch-limo
of a stroller and Casey by my side, picking off in my mind all the things I
could buy with one month's board. (I *know* you've done this, too.) But what

a hollow fantasy, in the end: A home filled with Jil Sander suits and Kosta Boda glassware doesn't mean anything if it doesn't also have a few pair of Devon-Aire breeches and some polo wraps under its roof.

"Will you just buy the horse already!" my husband implores.

"I don't think we should."

"You know we're gonna end up buying him anyway. Just do it!"

"We can't afford him. Besides, we don't have time to keep the house stocked with fresh milk. We have time for a horse?"

What is wrong with this guy, anyway? I think to myself. This is not normal spouse behavior. Husband from heaven? No. A forty-year-old ex-jock who considers my riding *his* last vicarious chance for athletic immortality. No problem! I'll take support any way I can.

But, support or no, this wasn't an easy decision. I knew the toll it would take on my family. But I also knew that without riding in my life, I'm a little like flat soda. And John knows it, too; it's part of the reason he urges me on. When I come home after a good ride and swing my kids into the air (John's way too big), their hearts sing along with mine.

Still, truth be told, there *are* more important things in life than riding. And it's the perspective those things provide that keeps us from selfishness and self-indulgence in deciding whether to go for the brass ring.

So there I am the other morning, sitting on the steps, lacing up my muddy paddock boots, one day after our bedroom closet collapsed entirely and the basement flooded. And John starts laughing and laughing and laughing. He's saying, "You gotta put this in your column! You gotta put this in your column!" And he's talking about the fact that neither of us is headed upstairs to take the tumbling bunches of wrinkled clothing off the fallen racks, and neither of us is headed downstairs with a mop and bucket. We're off to the barn!

It hasn't even been a week yet since we bought the horse, and the craziness has begun. I wouldn't have it any other way.

Here we go again.

DOCTOR, HEAL THYSELF? NAH.

It was an inauspicious beginning to a long week. *"Jan-nett! What kind of bit is that in your horse's mouth?!"* bellowed the singular voice of George Morris, whose clinic I was attending in Gladstone, New Jersey, during the Festival of Champions.

"An inadequate one," I confessed as my horse ran me all over the field.

"To-mor-row I want him in a slow twist!"

All right, a five-and-a-half-inch slow-twist snaffle by tomorrow morning, which meant finding one between the time I would return home from the clinic that afternoon (4:15 p.m.) and the time I had to be at the university to teach my graduate psychology seminar (4:30 p.m.).

"John," I said on the drive home, "I need you to get me a new bit tonight."

Traumatized once by having been sent out to buy me pantyhose (Reinforced toe? Sandalfoot? Control top? Jet black or off-black or did you want silky-sheer off-jet-black with reinforced, sandalwood-scented toe controls, dear?), John made sure not to be left high and dry again.

"Call the store and tell them to have it ready—because once they start asking me about eggs and butts, I'm lost."

Fair enough. I called in my order just as John dropped me off to teach in my boots and breeches and baseball cap. I tried to slip past the faculty office unnoticed, wondering how I was going to explain my duds to the semicircle of students I was about to face.

One day later, though, and Agassi and I had learned to gallop over banks, jump through grobs, and pull up(!). Four days later, we were winning the Festival's Equine Journalists' Show-Jumping National Championship. A lovely weekend indeed, it turned out.

But if you think for a moment that, by virtue of my profession, I escape the psychological maladies of horse showing, read on. The names, places, and dates change, but the mental side of showing remains the mental side of showing.

First, there are show nerves. To wit, I meet Mandy (Lorraine, *Practical Horseman*'s editor) and Sandra (Cooke, articles editor) at the Festival and they ask me if I'm nervous.

"Of course I'm nervous!" I respond. "Why do you think I have so much to say about the topic in my articles?"

Nothing too obvious to the casual observer, of course. Never mind that I've gone over my course thirty times, and never mind that when I say to Mandy, nearly an hour before my class, "Well, I guess I should start getting him ready," and she agrees, I start to panic. You see, I'm usually so early getting my horse ready (irrationally so) that if she (a rational person) is agreeing, I figure I must really be late. That kind of nervous.

Second, there's the feeling that I never have quite enough help at the show. I have one groom and her name is Janet. Sometimes I get a groom named John, although I don't know why I keep him on the payroll.

"Jan, I don't think he's listening to me. Why isn't he listening to me?" my husband wonders aloud at the far end of a loosely held lead shank.

"If you're asking, the answer is obvious," I reply.

In fact, the *only* reason I enter the ring in any sort of respectable shape on this tropically humid day of the journalists' class—during which I am stabled in one of the lower-rent stalls (no extra charge for the creek in front of the stall door)—is the generous help provided impromptu by Mandy and Sandra.

I think, though, that they just don't want to be embarrassed.

And then last but certainly not least is . . . the guilt! John is in New Jersey for the day earning a living (so that I can spend it) and the kids are (once again) spending Saturday afternoon with their sitter. And I'm at a "Festival"—yippee. Is there a better formula for guilt than that? I don't think so.

Heal thyself? I don't know. I'm not sure there's something to heal. To think about? Maybe. Change? I suppose so—it would be nice. But healing implies ailment. Somehow I've come to believe that these bugaboos of anxiety, nerves, guilt are part of being a competitor, part of being human.

[CHAPTER 6]

Buying Them
and Losing Them

JOSEPH'S STORY

We dream from childhood of how the horse of our own will look. Mine was a slender lad, dark brown, with four white socklets and a snip. It took me four horses and three decades to get a horse with even one white foot, and I rejoiced about that almost more than about the horse himself. Gone were the days of painting socks onto my horse's pictures; gone, the days of cutting off the toes of tube socks and sliding them up over humdrum pasterns. I was happy to do what other people did as a matter of unenthusiastic duty: haul out the pail, the sponge, and the Quic Silver, and scrub.

Montie's preconceptions were more practical—ability, size, presence. After all, she was looking for a dressage prospect; I (at least initially) had been looking for my version of Black Beauty. Here is Montie's endearing story of how the prejudice we disguise as romantic vision comes back to laugh in our faces.

"Joseph's story began months before I ever saw him, when a trainer at the race track asked if I wanted to see a chestnut horse she thought would be a cute show prospect. I asked how old (seven) and how big (15.3 hands), and told her I needed something much younger and bigger. I never went to look. After all, he didn't sound like a Real Dressage Prospect—you know, a great big horse, an elegant dark brown, something like that. . . .

"Months later, I was at that track photographing horses for this very trainer. When Mindy led Four Joe out, I knew he must be the one she'd wanted me to see earlier. He was gorgeous, but by now she was crazy about him — and, of course, he was too old and too small. . . .

"Days later, Mindy told me of wanting once again to sell Joe. It seems he'd broken on top the evening before and led all the way down to the quarter pole but then just stopped running. She wanted to find him a home before he broke down.

"I took her number and told her I'd call a friend. After all, Joe was too old and too small, and he certainly was not a Real Dressage Prospect. Perhaps, Nina, who was much smaller than I, would like him.

"But I was the one who came the next day to take a look. And the minute I picked up the reins on Joe, I knew he was right. He carried me faithfully through the pandemonium of a fifty-horse racing barn in the morning, and by evening we were headed home for a trial. So what if he wasn't a Real Dressage Prospect? I didn't care any more.

"During Joe's tryout, I found I could clip him and lead him alone and ride him safely out in the fields. He was fun.

"I took Joseph to a clinic eighteen days after his last race. At the end of our session, my coach turned to me and said, '*What do you mean, "not a Real Dressage Prospect"? This horse is your early birthday present from God!*' She insists that an angel whispered in Joseph's ear as he came close to that quarter pole, in that last race of his 105-race career, telling him to stop running, that a better life was out there for him."

Indeed it was.

Riding safely in the fields? Carrying faithfully? Fun? These are not the descriptions I hear from the many overmounted, overfaced, unhappy riders I talk with—riders on big, green horses that were just too pretty, too talented, too scopey, too whatever to pass up. Sure, he has a lot of potential—under a pro. Sure, she's pretty—but she's a maniac. And sure, he's going to be a big star—long after his owner/rider has given up the sport because of too many falls, near-misses, and times he didn't want to go to the barn any more. There are just too many (typically adult-amateur) riders whose naiveté, blind spot, bad judgment, wishful thinking, or ego has led down an unfortunate path to fear, injury, or discouragement.

Turn the page to read about the rationales that make so many people pass over the kinder, gentler, older, plainer, smaller horses who want to carry them faithfully, keep them safe, help them have fun. Maybe, like Montie, you'll end up with not just the right one, but the one you'd hoped for in the first place.

JOSEPH'S STORY, PART 2: FINDING A HORSE YOU CAN LIVE WITH

The previous story about Joseph, Montie's beloved new horse—the one she took a pass on at first, figuring mistakenly that he was not a Real Dressage Prospect—highlighted a little problem we have in the matchmaking end of this industry. Good marriage brokers we seem not to be, what with the numbers of people who are nervous about riding the very horses they bought to enjoy.

Some of these problems come from bad luck or bad advice or an overly enthusiastic trainer or an unscrupulous dealer or—omigosh—from our own blind spots. Want to hear some of the rationales behind bad matches?

"A young horse was all I could afford." This is like buying an assemble-it-yourself car kit for your first car because you couldn't afford a real one. Since when would you so readily sacrifice safety for cost? Look longer, or trim your wish list.

"I wanted something I could take to indoors once I learned to ride." Any horse that's going to really teach you how to ride isn't going to any indoors—and vice versa.

"My trainer said that a schoolmaster would cost more than what I have to spend." Schoolmaster as in retiring Grand-Prix-level horse? Yup. But schoolmaster as in quiet, sane, educated chum? I don't think so.

How do we get into these situations?

• **Naiveté.** I was fifteen when my parents and I bought my first horse—and even though I had a trainer at the time, I never picked up on the fact that you get your trainer's input before you buy. Imagine his surprise when I showed up with my brand-new horse (a cripple).

• **Insecurity.** We sure do wish to be part of something big and grand; if we can't find it in ourselves, we try to find it in those with whom we associate. So we pick a horse that soothes our ego but roughs up our bones and nerves.

• **Blind spots.** "'Hangs his legs in the air,' you say? I didn't see him hang his legs over those jumps. I'm sure it was just the angle you were watching him from. He jumps fine." When we really want something, we can do all kinds of mental gymnastics so nothing rains on our parade.

• **Too much deference.** "I had a feeling he was going to be too much horse for me, but I just didn't speak up. After all, she's the professional and I'm just a student. What do I know?" You know a lot. You know you better than anyone else—what feels right to you and what doesn't. Got a funny feeling in your belly? You've probably got a funny situation going down.

What to do differently?

• **Before you go shopping, educate yourself—about yourself.** Where does your personality make you vulnerable? Do you sometimes not look at what you don't want to see? Do you become coy and unassertive? Make a point of staying on top of what you think and feel, and find a way to make it part of the conversation. Cute belongs in a lead-line class, not in the decision-making process of an adult springing for a major purchase. Do you avoid conflict at all costs? Be prepared to articulate your point of view, listen to another perspective, change your mind, stand your ground, wade through some tension. Conflict isn't the worst thing in the world—certainly no worse than buying an unsuitable horse.

• **Listen hard, and then harder, to the voice inside that keeps saying something you don't like hearing.**

• **Take your time.** If you know you become impatient and impulsive, compensate up front by committing yourself to wait a certain amount of time at each juncture of the process before deciding anything. If you know you dislike indecision, insert "holds" on yourself that make you slow down. Figure you're kind of like a horse who needs rocks in his feed tub to slow down his gulping.

The point is to take care of your stuff so that it doesn't get in the way of your selecting the right horse for your needs and abilities and goals. We are all entitled to our quirks, but not at the expense of choosing the right partners for ourselves.

BUT I MIGHT RUIN HER

A girl of fifteen sits in my office, next to her mom. Dale comes because she gets too nervous at shows, too uptight during lessons, too intense around the barn. Her trainer admonishes her for trying too hard, yet yells at her when she makes a mistake. She takes it all to heart, trying harder the next time, and winds up making even more of a mess of things. Training deteriorates; her horse begins stopping; she rides increasingly defensively; the trainer rolls her eyes; mom is distraught.

Ever the perfectionist, Dale tries—of course—to be the perfect sport-psychology client as well. She comes eager for some relaxation routine she can execute at just the right moment before shows or lessons, or some visualization exercise she can dispatch prior to her children's jumper classes.

I tell her, instead, that our job is to make her a better *im*perfectionist, and that as much as I am aware she came hoping to learn how to be more perfect, I will offer her only something else.

"This will be," I tell her, "your biggest riding challenge. You might have thought it was your eye or your courage or even your horse. But you've become hostage to your fear of making mistakes, and it's eating away at your riding like a virus."

"But I don't know how *not* to try so hard," Dale replies.

"I know," I answer.

One week later, Dale, her mom, and I are again sitting together. Dale contrasts the anxiety with which she rides at her show barn to the confidence with which she rides at home, in her yard. Her horse there is a comfortable old soul, happy with a hack in the field. No great plans await him. But many plans await Anastasia, her young talent. And although Dale has established over the years a justly deserved and unanimously held reputation as a bold, tactful, get-the-job-done rider, on this new mare of hers—her first fancy one—she has become paralyzed. "I'm worried I'll ruin her," she says.

In rushes mom. "No, you won't," she promises. "She'll be fine! Don't worry about ruining her."

"She might," I say.

They turn abruptly and stare. *What did you say? Did we hear you right?*

"She might ruin her. We can't say. Nobody knows how many misses a horse has in her—some more, some less. But as long as you're captain, Dale, be captain, for better or for worse. You're a good rider, but you're only as good as you are. You owe her not a professional's ride, only a kind ride, an honest one. Anything more is gravy."

Dale's nervousness isn't about horse shows at all, really. It's about whether she'll be able to step up to the plate and deliver on a promise she never made and doesn't owe.

Having a nice horse does that to people. It did to me, until I learned to accept the risk of having it *not* work out. Once I began to let go of the expectation that I must not, no matter what, do any harm to my horse's fancy training or fancy talent or fancy whatever, my riding became more effective—as surely as will Dale's. People stop making the repeated mistakes that ruin horses *once they are given permission to make the mistakes that ruin horses*. Because they're no longer tied up in knots worrying about it, they stop riding defensively. The freedom to be human again paradoxically keeps both their good riding *and* the new horse intact.

Back in the '70s I watched a little mare, Grey Mist, win everything in sight in the hunter ring under Buddy Brown. Then she was sold to a junior. At their first show together everybody, including me, gathered around the ring to see how they'd fare. The poor girl crashed. Really, how else could she have done, given the pressure? Soon thereafter they got it together, but it must have been so difficult for that girl to walk into and out of that ring.

No one wants to ruin a horse—any horse. But there is no truer or more genuine way out of this dilemma than to accept the inherent risk and at the same time try to rise to the occasion.

Demands for excellence? No problem. Anyone—trainers and myself alike—can ask that of me. Just don't ask for perfect. I don't do that anymore. And, of course, since I've stopped, everything seems to happen that much more easily.

There is such a thing as being too careful. Too-careful horses lose their hearts. Too-careful people do, too.

LOSING A GOOD ONE

L osing any animal that's been an important part of our lives is difficult. No matter the personality quirk, the variable obedience, the funny look—in having cared for them and in having let them care for us in their own imperfect ways, we grew attached. We miss them when they go, we mourn, and, after a while, we move on.

But once or twice, maybe more if we're lucky, our paths cross with an animal who's pretty special. He's not so easy to let go, and it's not so easy to move on. That's what happened to Valerie:

. . . A few months back, my horse, with whom I had a very special bond, colicked. He didn't make it through surgery. Now, no matter how hard I try, I cannot seem to get past this. I miss him terribly and am unsure what to do now. Riding now just doesn't feel like the same activity. . . . The more time that goes by, the easier it becomes to skip the barn altogether. My trainer feels I should get another horse. . . . My worst fear is that the very thing that made my horse so special—the love and commitment and bond— is the thing that will never happen again.

You miss your guy, Valerie, and will for a long while. He was a friend, and his loss, just like that of a human friend, has left a big empty ache.

What now? Maybe nothing for a little while, maybe something different. Riding *won't* be the same as long as that's what you're waiting for it to be. Let riding be whatever it's going to be now until you recognize how you can love it again, even if it is different.

You wonder, too, if the time has come to look for another horse. Again maybe, maybe not. One way to discover how ready you are is to begin looking and then see if your heart's in it. If you go out looking and feel dull about the whole thing, put it off for a month or two and try it again. If you go out looking and feel sad about it *but excited about the prospect of finding someone new*, that's OK—keep looking. When you're bereaved, you must give yourself permission to feel sad about what's lost *and* to be excited simultaneously for a future that you are lucky enough still to have in front of you. We don't have to finish with one feeling in order to go on to the next.

There's something else I want to say to you. And it's that you were a major part of making that relationship between you and your horse so special. It didn't "just happen," and it wasn't all him. He may have brought his own magic, but you recognized it, and you made room in your life for it, and for him. If you were able to do that once, Valerie, you can do it again. With someone new. The thing is, as with the riding, to allow the new relationship to be a different one. Just as strong, just as special—but different. In our more philosophical moments, John, my husband, tells me that were I ever to lose him, I must allow myself to fall in love again—just as richly, just as intensely—*but* with someone I would love for reasons different from those for which I love him. We are each an original.

Take your time to mourn. You'll know how long that time needs to be. Don't let anyone else pressure you into shortchanging yourself because your loss was "just an animal." Don't delude yourself into thinking that *doing something* (anything) is a better option than simply doing nothing for a while and feeling sad. At the same time, don't think that you must wait until you feel "all better" to begin adding new pieces to your life. Use this period to learn more about your personal needs in times of crisis and loss, and to respect them. You owe no one an answer about what you are going to do. If people ask, tell them honestly that you don't know yet, and that you're trying to figure it out.

Most important, Valerie, always remember that your contribution to that special bond with your horse is something you still carry with you. When you're ready, you can share it again. When you're ready, you'll *want* to.

[CHAPTER 7]

Self and Body Image

CONFIDENCE LOST AND FOUND

Ever feel you're not the rider you once were? Haley did: *I've ridden since I was six; from my eleventh birthday on, I passed my days at the barn. Last year, riding fell into a rut—wasn't learning much in my lessons, felt bad about how the lesson horses were treated. I stayed away, busying myself with college applications.*

A year later and ten pounds heavier, I'm finally ready to get back into riding. The good news is that soon I'll be starting at a small college with a lovely barn nearby. The bad news is that my extended absence from the sport has cost me my confidence. If only I still felt like a rider! Emotionally, I've begun to doubt I ever was a rider. But I do know that I miss riding, and that I don't want to let the psychological nitty-gritty of my re-initiation interfere with my having the equine time of my life.

I know, Haley, that popular sport culture is always warning us to "use it or lose it." But that "it"—muscle tone—is only part of your riding self. Think of your general fund of knowledge about horses, your riding experiences, and your attitudes about learning. These more strongly (and more permanently) define who you are as a rider. And they are still with you. They never left you, Haley, even when you left the sport. Let me see if I can help you relax about your year away and trace the part of you that continued to be a rider while you were miles from a saddle.

LEARNING IN SURPRISING WAYS

Eighteen years ago, I learned transcendental meditation. One piece of its wisdom has always stuck with me: that mental (and physical) skills will often consolidate during time away from the activity being learned. I began to understand why, after breaks from riding because of school, work, and travel, I returned to the ring in some ways a better rider than when I'd left it. (More recently, after motherhood, the same thing happened again.)

Don't let your time away from riding get you spooked, Haley. You were still a rider all that time. You just weren't riding. There's a big difference.

Besides, you may find that some things you learned in the year away are very valuable in your riding. Inadvertently, I'm learning a lot about riding by raising my little boys. I'm learning diplomacy and patience. I'm learning the art of negotiation. I'm learning about living with less control than I mistakenly believed I had. I use it all in the riding ring.

How have you grown in the past year? What did you learn about yourself or about relationships or about being more tolerant or more forgiving or more assertive or less perfectionistic? Take a moment, Haley, to find one personal attribute that evolved, or one special experience that took place, and consider how it could be useful to you as a rider. These growth areas are as important as technique—or even more, I'd argue—to your full development as an athlete.

CLOSER THAN YOU THINK

Haley, I also wonder if you are making negative assumptions about yourself as a returning rider and treating them as truths. I'm not a fan of false affirmations; I don't want you standing in front of a mirror trying to convince yourself that you are confident. But it's possible that confidence is right around the corner for you, and that a flexible, positive attitude (coupled with a graduated re-entry into riding, patient instructors, and quiet, confidence-building school horses) can have you believing in yourself within a couple of rides. Just be careful about trying to jump-start your comeback with too big a ride (challenging horses and lessons); such efforts to "prove" to yourself that you are the rider you were could backfire big-time. Starting off slowly will get you there faster.

One more thing, Haley: Pick out three or four of your favorite riding memories and soak in them as you would in a warm bath. Keep them nearby in your thoughts, and use them again and again to awaken your sense of yourself as a rider with more than a decade of experience. Been away for a year? So have esteemed teachers on sabbatical. They come back better than ever. You have twelve marvelous years of riding under your belt. Don't let them get intimidated by one punky year off.

IN OUR OWN BACKYARD

I just heard about three college wrestlers who died trying to "cut weight." Hoping to squeeze into lower weight categories for upcoming competitions, these nice guys deprived themselves of food and water and subjected themselves to steam rooms and extravagant exercise routines. They lost the game—big-time.

Our own community of riders isn't immune to eating disorders. Among us, it's mainly juniors and young adult women—occasionally an older adult—who exhibit preoccupations with food, undergo striking fluctuations in weight, and conceal induced vomiting, laxative abuse, and/or self-starvation.

We don't talk about it much; not talking about problems is old hat in this hushed industry of ours. We're going to need to *start* talking, though, as the issue tugs harder and harder at the sleeves of parents, friends, and trainers who find themselves becoming reluctant witnesses to a loved one's physical, and sometimes psychological, deterioration.

But this is hard. . . . After all, who should say something? In general, I suppose, an individual's weight should be the business of no one but herself and those she chooses to discuss it with. But when the person in question is young, or is endangered, all that changes. The people who matter to her, and to whom she matters, are the ones who must step up to the plate and speak.

And if you're one of those people, what should you say? The truth. Say that you're worried, say you've noticed changes, say you'll help her to get help, say you will not give up on her. If a kid is getting too thin, or developing bizarre eating habits (e.g., eating only a small salad once a day), or if she regularly runs off to the bathroom after eating a full meal and stays there, tell her—without judgment or criticism—that you are worried she is having problems with her eating.

Don't, by the way, bank on logic to help you; it holds little currency in the court of eating disorders. It's *not logical* for people to starve themselves to death. But they do. Every day, mothers and fathers and sisters and brothers and friends, unknowingly ill-armed with only love and logic, appeal to common sense as they try to reach the child or sibling or chum with an eating disorder. But the callous forces of anorexia and bulimia are immune to such appeals; accusing internal echoes of *You're still too fat!* can always drown out a mother's loving, panicked call.

Anorexia is so dangerous because it takes people to their deaths smiling. By eating only so much, these young women (and, occasionally, men) acquire a sense of self that is physical, eloquent, powerful—a masterful self-control. *I feel fine*, they assure you. And they do. It's only you and the rest of the world who see the ravished body.

There are ways, however, to combat this insidious disorder. For starters, don't be shy. Get professional help as soon as you notice a problem. Mandate help if the kid's a minor. If you're a parent who suspects a problem, speak to your child's physician. Ask if your worries are warranted. Let the doctor play the heavy. Ask for a referral for therapy. You can also get good referrals from your state psychological association. Or from local universities. Or from friends—word-of-mouth referrals are usually the best.

Another way to combat this problem up front is by being careful about what we tell our young riders about weight management. Slender may be some people's ideal, but it's not everybody's body. Parents and trainers who thought they didn't need to speak directly about weight control—just as they didn't think they needed to speak about sportsmanship or responsibility—may find themselves needing to take on the role of educator.

Incidentally, when I was seventeen, I hid from my trainer whenever I ate, fearing his scrutiny over my choice of food. I never developed an eating problem, but I remember feeling as guilty as my friend who hid her cigarettes from him. Her cigarettes! Imagine that. All I was doing was eating lunch.

WHERE LEAN IS QUEEN

Dear Janet: I've been riding for five years as an adult . . . recently found a wonderful instructor . . . but still have problems. I can bend unbendable school horses, sit the trot without stirrups for hours, jump fairly well from a brisk trot. . . . I just don't canter very well. —Lilly

Unless the transition is smooth and easy, Lilly ends up perching, pulling, or whizzing around the ring at a forty-five-mph trot. She attributes a lot of her problem to her being overweight and wonders if other heavy riders have similar difficulties. Lilly says she recognizes that diet and exercise could improve her riding, but she wonders what she "could do psychologically to convince myself of my abilities and help myself to ride better *as I am now*."

Lilly, you are far from alone. I've received several similar letters. Most poignant, perhaps, was one from a woman who quit riding because she kept getting what she called the "raised eyebrow." She'd returned to riding after many years away and, no longer ninety-five pounds, found her battles with weight an added trial in the learning process and an unappreciated one on the parts of her trainer and riding buddies.

Two issues come to light here. The first is that of developing a self-affirming identity as a rider—one that realistically balances your own ability and resources with the limitations extra weight imposes on the athletic endeavor of riding. The second is the discouragement and psychological pain that you might, like the other letter-writer, suffer at the hands of insensitive peers, instructors, and perhaps strangers, too.

For many people, the way out of these conundrums is robust self-acceptance that both fuels enthusiasm for what you're doing and can serve as the emotional "anesthesia" you need to carry on. But the most serviceable kind of self-acceptance recognizes limitations. Extra weight—like very short legs, or a budget that can afford only a horse of moderate talent, or work and family obligations that permit riding only twice a week—means that certain aspects of riding will be more difficult to nail down. You acknowledge and make do with what you have until you can manage something different. Fortunately, because mental factors play such a large role in riding, you can compensate for handicaps of body size or type, limited funds, or limited time by means of psychological skills such as attitude, judgment, perceptiveness, receptiveness to instruction, decision-making, and the like: skills you can learn or, if you already have them, refine.

How about for those who don't have a supportive external riding environment? I'd suggest you seek a trainer who'll openly support your riding as you are now. And the best way to determine that is to ask forthrightly when you first discuss working together, saying something along these lines: "I'm aware certain trainers are not comfortable teaching heavier riders. I'm overweight; would you have a problem with teaching me?" If you can, have this conversation over the phone, if only to avoid any potential self-consciousness when you first meet in person.

As for the raised eyebrows—well, there will always be those who feel entitled to comment, by word or body language. Sharp wit comes in handy here, or simply a response like "I would appreciate it if you'd please keep any concerns you have about my body size to yourself." Just be sure not to add your own self-critical voice or brow to those of others. Focus on what you do well on and around horses, and on your commitment to your sport; nobody can take those from you. In that context, you can transform overcoming weight-related riding problems, and/or even losing weight, into further riding goals—much like the goals of developing a deeper seat, a better eye, or a more patient approach to a fence. (This perspective is similar to one I sometimes suggest if a rider says she can't "make" her show nerves go away; rather than fighting them, she learns to incorporate them into her landscape of riding challenges, making them another thing to learn to manage more effectively over time.)

The important thing is to abolish—through your own self-acceptance and *your* sense of "belonging" in the equestrian community—the embarrassment and even self-disdain some overweight riders feel. I don't know of anyone who's ever ridden better by chiding herself (or being chided) for her size.

ON BEING A PREGNANT RIDER

I'm becoming more and more round, and it's not because I'm any softer in my mouth. I am, however, softer in my muscles, and in my belly, and in my silhouette. As I move along in this—my second—pregnancy, I watch my transformation from athlete to expectant mother/sideliner with a coupled sense of suspense and disquiet.

Last year at this time I was gearing up for the season with a brand-new horse and brand-new set of expectations. I was lean and mean and ready to roll. It's strange, now, not to be thinking of myself as an athlete. I don't feel like one, and I know I don't move around like one. I don't go up stairs like one, or get in and out of cars the way an athlete does. Instead, I'm out of breath after walking to my office from the parking lot—a quarter the distance of courses I used to gallantly stride off.

But as important as my riding has been to me, my husband and I wanted another child and chose to take off this year to do that. That it will affect my riding more than his is a biological given. That I will return to the sport as mentally fit as I left it is not.

When our son, Casey, was born three and a half years ago, I waited my six weeks and got right back into the saddle. Sure, I had to grab mane to stay in my two-point, and my legs swung like metronomes, but I was riding again. To be honest, I think I was more pleased about having followed through with my public (and all too cavalier) proclamations during the pregnancy that I'd be showing (horses, that is, not abdomen) "within three months of delivery" than I was about riding again itself.

This go-round, I'm more modest. It might be that I'm a few years older. It might be that I feel myself changing in ways that are yet unrecognizable to me. Or it might be that I'm worried my intense desire to train and to show will have growing competition from the pull of three little faces (yes, it's twins!) and one big one looking to do something "normal" on a

Saturday or Sunday. John, my husband, has always been nothing but encouraging, but will I be able to see through my own guilt about commandeering so much of our family's resources for my riding to even recognize his support? Even more frightening to me is the thought that the competition would come largely from within myself—that *I* would want to do something more, you know, "normal" on the weekend. And what if I just don't want riding as badly as I did before? What if I do but just can't make it work the way I could with only one in tow? With three kids, John and I are outnumbered. . . . Everything will change.

But there's something else, too: the level of risk I'll be comfortable assuming when I start up again. I have no idea why it would be any different with three children than with one, but I worry that I could reassess and come up with narrower limits. I do remember standing on deck at different in-gates last summer, sizing up jumpoffs, preparing myself to go in and do my job. And then I'd occasionally get this thought: Don't forget, Janet, Casey needs a mother. Now what in the world was I supposed to do with *that* while galloping into the ring? How does any rider—jumper or otherwise—reconcile concern for the welfare of loved ones with a desire to ride aggressively and win? What will I think next year at these in-gates? And what will John be thinking? After all, if things get ugly for me, he's left in charge.

This past winter, I enjoyed being benched (doctors said no riding once twins were detected). I'd smile my smug smile as John, a recent convert to this sport, went dutifully into the blistering cold to ride. I'd turn up the heat and settle a little more deeply into the sofa. And since the decision about when to stop riding wasn't even mine, I didn't have to feel like some sort of equestrian lightweight for not riding all the way up to my due date or something crazy like that.

See, but now spring has come—and instead of laughing at my husband, I've begun to feel like the hound left behind for the first run of the season. *I want to go, too!* I feel like yelling out. I go to my mailbox hoping for some nice reading magazines but find it stuffed with prize lists. *Don't you people know I can't go? Why do you do this to me?!?* The lists go on John's side of the desk now, a few novice eq classes highlighted for him, instead of my amateur-owner jumper classics and mini prixes. The irony of all this is hardly lost on me—after all, I turned him on to riding in the first place; here he is trotting off to lessons and shows while I get my fixes from an occasional ESPN show-jumping special and hearing the stories he comes home with.

Someone at a seminar I gave last week asked if I wasn't concerned that these new babies would affect my riding. "They already have!" I replied. And in the quiet of my drive home I became aware of the split screen that's established itself in my head, half reflecting the part of me that is adamant about making it all work—finding time to ride, getting to shows, moving up to bigger amateur classes—and half reflecting my lack of certainty, my growing ambivalences. I hate that latter screen, and I'm saddened to think things could go in a way other than the one I'd been anticipating. There's a big difference between positive thinking and Pollyanna.

There are only the questions for now for me, no answers yet. But in the privacy of a consultation or therapy session, or in the conversational flow of a seminar, I hear other riders, parents, and parents-to-be bumping up against these same questions. Often what had seemed a riding problem turns out to be an underground, unspoken worry about how to balance family, career, and sporting life, or about how natural life changes will affect one's body, one's mind. It's a far more communal experience than most of us recognize.

Oh, and yes, we do know—two little boys!

WEIGHTY MATTERS

Y ou come home, slam your keys on the kitchen table, and sit down in a huff. "If she says one more word about my weight, I'll . . . I'll . . ."

"You'll what?" wonders your spouse/ friend/daughter/dad.

"I'll . . . SAY something!" you reply, shoulders collapsing and spirits sagging as you recall just how many times you've made this promise.

"I just never know *what* to say," you add. "I think of something later, but it always sounds stupid or too defensive. I'm afraid it'll just make things worse."

If this sounds like you—one of so many searching for a better way to manage unwelcome comments about your body size, read on. Yours, incidentally, is a vastly different situation from that of the eating-disordered youngsters I wrote of in a previous column, who, when health and especially life are threatened, may require aggressive outside intervention— even over their protests. Your situation affects looks more than immediate health, and it's not so clear whose—if anyone's—business (other than yours) it is.

Yet some people *make* it their business. Among them is the occasional riding instructor who feels that any student, by virtue of being in a training program, opens herself up to discussions of weight as it affects either the execution or the aesthetics of her riding.

I disagree. Trainers, I believe that unless a student directly asks for your opinion or the horse is uncomfortable, weight is solely her business. It's not as though she doesn't know her own body size and shape. But her feelings about them may differ from yours—reflecting maybe culture, family history, or other factors of which you are unaware.

I find it helpful to figure that, at any given point in their lives, people are usually doing the best they can or want to with the energy, time, and resources they have. The fact is we don't all make the same decisions about things. And although a student's decisions about her weight may *matter* to her friend or parent or instructor, the truth is that her weight is not under their control. To treat it as if it were is unproductive.

"But Janet," I'm often challenged, "what about the heavier rider who can't keep her balance and snatches her horse's mouth or flops onto his back?" These are legitimate concerns—but they aren't weight issues. They're *horsemanship* issues. We see these faults all the time for reasons that have nothing to do with weight.

The fact is that some heavy riders ride quietly and some light riders do not. It's really the rider's responsibility to educate herself to ride kindly—by whatever means best suit her. That may be by losing weight, but it can also be by more training, better instruction, or greater fitness.

Now let's turn back to you, that student who keeps promising to "say something." Here are some ideas that will neither blow the other person out of the water nor leave you feeling like a chump.

As it's happening: "Michael, enough. I don't find what you're saying funny."

If the reply is *Oh, don't be so sensitive*, come right back with "Michael, I'm not being sensitive. I'm being firm."

If the reply is *Oh, don't take everything so personally. I tell everyone to lose weight,* say, "It's personal when you say it to me. Enough."

After the fact: "Lucy, the comments you make about my weight during my group lessons embarrass me. Please stop." Or "That doesn't help me, Steve. Your remarks only make it worse."

Having the words in front of you is the first (and easier) step. Now you need to step up to the plate and act on your own behalf. Don't wait around hoping your instructor will read your mind, or figure out you're unhappy from your scowl, or respond to your silent treatment; those are ineffective strategies. Speak up thoughtfully and clearly. Presenting your concerns forthrightly and calmly invites others to treat you in a similarly dignified manner. If you've ever wondered what you could do to change how people act toward you, consider doing something that reflects a different statement about who you are.

I DON'T SHAVE ON SATURDAYS

When I temporarily hung up my spurs during the latter months of my first pregnancy, seven years ago, my husband, John, thought it would be a good time to start riding and see what all the fuss was about. After all, we had (at that time) a not-too-fancy, not-too-green, not-too-quirky little hunter who had no job now that I wasn't riding.

"Jan, let me take one of those lessons on Tim where you go around on a rope."

"Go for it."

John comes home from that first lesson and announces that he's signed up for nine more. "I'm going to do a set of ten. That'll be enough. Then I'll know what's what when you're riding again."

Nine lessons later, John decides to stay on for a while. "OK with you, Jan? Tim seems happy, and Gaye says I'm doing really well!"

I dreamily roll onto the other side of my big ol' belly and murmur approval: "Knock yourself out." What are a few more lessons?

Six months later, I'm taking John shopping in preparation for his first horse show. He is trying on jackets and asking the attendant why he should get more dressed up to compete in a sporting event than to go to work as a psychologist. The attendant smiles and shows him some nice dress shirts.

John is just beginning to understand how different showing a horse is going to be from playing rugby and football—what he used to do on Saturdays. He wants to know where you spit.

"You don't," I warn him.

"Do we all smash our hunt caps together in a pre-show huddle?"

"Stop." I also tell him to refrain from the cheers he'd been giving himself whenever he cleared a fence.

"What should I say instead?"

"Nothing."

"*Nothing?* Can I curse if I get the wrong lead?"

"John," I plead, "we live and work in this community. Our kids will attend school here. Be civilized."

"OK, I'll be good," he promises.

The following week, John—all six foot two and 230 pounds of him—is sitting on his horse by the in-gate of a local show, dressed to the nines and surrounded by a dozen or so small children on little horses and ponies, all waiting to enter the ring. It is a Beginner Rider class. John is making faces at the children—mean ones. His trainer asks what he's doing.

"I'm intimidating the opposition. How come they're not making faces at me?"

"John," his trainer educates, "you're *scaring* them. The judge wants to see polite riders. Try to have a pleasant look on your face. If you win a ribbon, lean down, pat your horse, and thank the official handing it to you."

Thank the official? John wonders.

So John trots in with a look that's not so much pleasant as it is puzzled. What kind of sport is this, where you can't spit or holler or growl at your adversary and you have to shower and shave and dress like you're going to a breakfast meeting?

A sport all its own, any one of us would tell him.

Oh, he's hooked now, of course: loves his weekly lessons, loves his once- or twice-a-year horse shows, waits for the day when he might have a horse of his own. I think he *got* hooked during that very first show: By his last jumping class, with only a handful of contenders left, John reigned supreme over those four crossrails—and as he took his victory gallop, his rugby self burst through. Up in the air went the fist, broad across his face spread the smile, and loud came the hoot from his mouth. It was fine, and everybody—kids, too—joined in. I guess you can take the man out of the game but . . . you know the rest.

These days, the more classically built riders with the right expressions all get pinned ahead of John, but he still intends an end run one day with an assault on the Chicken Little jumper division. Somehow, though, he and the sport are managing to meet in the middle: He grabs each new *Practical* when it arrives and opens it to George Morris's column, searching for examples of "proper" expressions and etiquette to emulate.

[CHAPTER 8]

Advice for Younger Riders

THREE THINGS KIDS NEVER TELL THEIR TRAINERS

Dear Janet: My daughter, Rachel, rides in the pony hunters. She's always loved lessons and showing. Recently, however, she seems to have so much on her mind, especially when she shows. Because she's become more competitive as a rider, she's been receiving more attention from her trainer. It's what she's always wanted (she idolizes her trainer), but she appears almost burdened by her own progress. I try to talk with her, but she has trouble expressing herself. Is this sort of thing common? Can you offer any insight on what she might be experiencing? —Sharon

Sharon, I've never met your daughter, but I've met hundreds like her—and I welcome this opportunity to shed light on what she may be going through. Read on for a description of three new emotions many such kids experience toward their trainers as their riding carries them to new levels of attention and expectations—all normal, but also uncomfortable. Ask Rachel if any of them ring true for her. And don't worry about placing blame for the pressure she's feeling; much of it is a natural consequence of competitive situations and competitive temperaments, anyway. Just work to help her to continue enjoying her riding and her talent—and to manage the emotional repercussions of advancing. That's as much a part of her learning as is the refining of her technical skills.

• **"I'm afraid to make mistakes and disappoint you when I ride."** Even if they don't say it, most young riders think the world of their trainers. It's hard-wired into the student/instructor (mentor) relationship—especially for young teenagers, whose allegiances shift from parents to adults outside the family as the adolescent bell for independence and separation tolls. So a trainer's opinion can affect a kid's self-confidence disproportionately.

Ask Rachel if she worries more now about disappointing her trainer, given her success. Remind her of all the things she is and does that make you and her trainer proud of her and that have nothing to do with performance outcomes. Give her frank permission to make mistakes—help break the trend in this industry to value "perfection" over effectiveness.

- **"I'm afraid I'll make mistakes in my riding and mess up my pony."** No kid—or grownup, for that matter—can ride well if she's thinking she has to give a "perfect" ride to prevent a bad thing from happening. What happens is she doesn't ride at all. She sits there trying not to make a mistake—and her horse or pony ends up wondering if anyone's aboard. The truth is that horses and ponies get messed up all the time. So do we. That's life. We all either learn to roll with the punches and recover, or we don't. Free your daughter from the impossible responsibility of not "ruining" her pony; do your best to make sure she's in a well-supervised program on a forgiving pony who's adored at least as much for his heart as for his perfect lead changes.

- **"Being a little 'special,' I feel terribly self-conscious around you, and I worry about saying or doing something stupid. Sometimes I get too shy even to talk."** This one has my name on it, Sharon. It's the 1970s. I'm sitting in the cab of a six-horse van that carries only my one chestnut mare. The show season is winding down, and I'm one win away from qualifying for the ASPCA Maclay Finals in Madison Square Garden. My trainer—the venerable, wonderful Wayne Carroll—is taking me all around New York and Connecticut, giving me a couple of last tries. He usually travels to shows with no less than a dozen riders, most of whom have already qualified, so I can't believe he's doing this just for me.

Wayne's merrily driving along, and I can't think of a thing to say—for hours. I feel transparent in our silence; I'm sure he can see my crush on him. I feel embarrassed and special at the same time. Such is the stuff of adolescence, and of wanting to do well for someone who thinks you're worth the extra attention.

Let Rachel know she's normal and wonderful and learning more than she knows. Assure her that she can talk to you any time, even if she doesn't know what she wants to talk about, and that the stresses she feels are real, even if she doesn't know what they are. Tell her she can take a break, not take a break, stumble, or soar, and you will always think the world of her and what she's trying to do.

DEALING WITH THE PARENT WHO YELLS

Janet, I have a parent who yells at her kid in front of others, both at the barn and at shows. It's horrible, and I don't know what to do or if I even have any business doing anything—after all, it's her kid. Help! —Sandy

In an earlier column, we heard from a trainer who had her hands full managing her teenage riders. In this letter, Sandy manages her teens all right but has a heck of a time with their parents!

I love this letter. It gives me a chance to rail against that ugly, ugly side of youth sports: adults yelling at children because they think the kids aren't trying hard enough. *Don't these grownups get it?*

Here's a story for you, Sandy, to get this topic rolling. Two evenings before I wrote this column, I did an eleventh-hour phone consultation with a young man headed into the Maclay Finals next morning. He was still smarting from the remark his dad welcomed him with as he stepped out of the ring at the Medal Finals two weeks before: "Aren't you tired of losing?"

This is supposed to help?

IT *IS* YOUR BUSINESS

Sandy, when a parent yells at one of your riders while that rider is working with you, it most certainly is your business. It became your business when the rider's parents asked you to be their child's trainer. Not only does a screaming parent reflect poorly on your business, but screaming is counterproductive, demeaning, and unsportsmanlike. It has no place in teaching.

(Make sure, though, that the pot isn't calling the kettle black! Your argument to such folks goes down the potty the moment *you*, while instructing, let fly with a remark that's cutting, sarcastic, or too many decibels too high. If you're guilty, discover some better ways to teach.

Sign on for one or two teaching clinics, read books on educating young people, and/or spend time studying and then modeling yourself on those teachers whose style you respect. Then you are free to ask your parents to change.)

Now, for that yeller of yours . . .

WHAT TO DO—VERSION 1

Approach the parent during a quiet, conflict-free moment. Make sure other people, including the child, are not around. Tell the parent that you understand how this sport can make for a lot of frustrations, *but* that you cannot allow her to reprimand the child publicly for riding errors. Explain that such a reprimand makes any child afraid to ride boldly because she becomes afraid of making mistakes and afraid of disappointing adults; that it fractures the rapport between parent and child; that it makes the child sad; and that it is not an acceptable part of your training program. Tell the parent that this kind of public reprimand can't happen again, and that you will ask her to have her child trained elsewhere if it continues.

Then be prepared to lose a client if the parent either doesn't care for or ignores your comments. No professional—in any field—can be effective or credible if she feels she can't afford to lose a client. You must have faith in your rapport and/or your history with the person, and in your judgment of the situation.

WHAT TO DO—VERSION 2

Another way to deal with this situation is less direct, softer, and uses humor. For some people and some barns, it's a better choice. And it suits a situation where there are several yellers.

What you do, Sandy, is hold a "Parents' Horse Show" at the barn. The parents all ride hobbyhorses—you know, those toys with fuzzy horse heads topping wooden poles. Moms and dads compete in a variety of classes, with their kids serving as their trainers: The kids warm the parents up, school them, put them in the ring. Caricature and hysteria are to be encouraged. Your barn manager is judge. *Your* job is to pass out awards for good sportsmanship. The parents will get the point.

PROOF IN THE PUDDING

A young rider wonders about making her Olympic dreams come true: *I'm twelve years old and just got my own horse. I ride every day and plan on getting good enough to ride in the Olympics. I'm very serious about this. But when I tell my instructor, she just smiles and tells me, "We'll see. . . ." My parents don't even smile—they just look at each other and roll their eyes. How can I get them all to take my riding more seriously? —Lindsay*

L indsay, the best way for you to get people to take your riding more seriously is for you to take it as seriously as you can. This means doing a lot of different things in your pursuit of your goal, only some of which actually involve sitting in the saddle. But first, the riding part.

Riding every day is great, but riding as many horses a day as possible is even better. Don't even think of being choosy about the rides you get (unless they're dangerous or too green for you), and don't complain about the horses you do get to ride. Aspiring but unproven riders like yourself often start at the back of the barn. Remember, too, that people are usually doing you a favor by giving you rides, no matter how old, ugly, pokey, or unfit. Close your eyes and mount up.

Another part of taking your riding and your goals seriously involves learning everything you can about horsemanship and about good horse and barn management. This means quietly following your trainer (you'll need a good one to usher you along this path) around as she oversees barn duties, so you can observe how she handles the different jobs, customers, horses, and employees. Any international-level competitor will tell you that a lot of how she or he has arrived—and stayed—at that level involves good management of her horses, her support people, her operation as a whole. Nobody rides for a country all by herself.

Besides working or volunteering time at your barn in order to learn how to do all the things involved in keeping horses and horse owners and riders happy, watch other instructors at horse shows, trials, club rallies, and the like to see how they might do things differently. Work out a summer internship with an equine veterinarian or equine chiropractor or certified massage therapist who works with horses to see up close how a horse-health-care professional works and contributes to the overall health and well-being of performance horses. And, of course, take as many lessons and clinics with as many different instructors as you can afford.

Can't afford all those lessons? Arrange to be a working student or to trade services. Are you willing to muck? Run errands? Groom? Baby-sit? Wash water buckets?

Once you get within earshot of someone who knows what she's doing, listen to what she says, even if you disagree—on second thought, especially if you disagree. Later on you'll have the time and wisdom to figure out which learnings you want to keep and which you don't.

Want to know the name of a great instructor? Mr. Schooling Ring. Low rates. Watch and listen to all those professionals work with their students and with their horses. Watch how the better students learn. Watch how they adjust their riding to their instructors' direction. See how the less-than-better ones don't.

Read. Rent videos. Read some more. No extra money for subscriptions? I still startle at how many riding books and magazines I see on the shelves of my local library. Good ones! New ones!

Actions always speak louder than words, Lindsay, and never is this more true than when somebody announces a desire to reach a high goal. If you want to go to the Olympics, stop worrying about whether or not other people are taking you seriously and start your program. Almost anybody will start to pay attention to—and take more seriously—the person who means what she says and shows it through what she does.

I AIN'T A KID ANYMORE

You know it's going to happen someday, but it's so gradual that you don't spot it until it's happened already: summers, holidays, people growing up.

A week ago I looked at my twins and realized with a jolt that they're no longer infants. Maybe it was Jake's hair looking less willy-nilly, or Austin's evolved facial structure, giving a first hint of how he'll look as a teenager. Two weeks shy of their first birthday, and just as they should, my babes have become boys.

The transition out of juniors has its markers, too. Each new year ushers bunches of old juniors into the amateur ranks. But that's a change in name only. Making the transformation to equestrian adulthood's responsibilities, roles, and relationships takes a little longer.

About a month ago, a client of mine in her early twenties was telling me about her experiences at a recent show. She does the bigger hunter classes, enjoys being competitive, and takes her training seriously, although not as intensively as when she was a junior. Speaking of her trainer, she sighed, saying that she loved the instruction but didn't enjoy being talked to as she'd been as a teenager: "I don't like being yelled at at shows. And I've heard enough comments that I'm not trying hard enough or not serious enough. That's just not acceptable to me now. It never really was, but when I was young I thought it was how you *had* to be trained if you were serious."

"Jess" isn't alone in having tolerated the yelling and screaming and belittlement, believing they came with the territory. Kids—and adults—put up with stuff they wouldn't *dream* of taking from someone who wasn't their trainer. Now, though, seemingly, she'd had a significant developmental shift. She was feeling the changes and was ready to live parts of her life a little differently. But the people around her didn't know that. (Should they have? Maybe, maybe not; more on that later.) So what Jess needed was a way to let her trainer know she felt differently about things and, to whatever extent was reasonable, wanted her training to reflect the change. Which meant speaking up. Oh boy.

"Have you mentioned any of this to your trainer?" I asked Jess.

"Oh, no. It's OK; it's really no big deal," she backpedaled.

"Well," I asked, "what *would* you say if you wanted to say something to change things?"

"I guess something like, 'You know, Ros, I like training with you, but I sometimes feel that you still treat me like a junior'"—as if juniors should be treated less courteously than adults!—"'and I don't feel like one anymore.'"

"What do you think Ros would say?"

"Well, she might look at me as if I was from outer space. . . . Or she might say, 'What do you mean?' And then I guess *I'd* say, 'I'd rather you didn't yell at me—it just makes me ride worse. And sometimes I worry you'll think I'm not serious if I don't come out and ride without irons three times a week and watch riding videos every night. I *am* still a serious rider, but I'm a different one.'"

Having imagined this dialogue with Ros, Jess could now practice saying out loud what she needed to say—practice saying it in different ways, even practice getting nervous and tongue-tied but still making her point. It didn't have to be pretty, just effective.

But there was one more point for Jess and me to talk about. I asked her how *she* might be adding to Ros's idea that she was the same old kid. Jess thought and said that perhaps in many ways she was still acting like the junior she'd been for six years with Ros: never really initiating any kind of conversation, and giggling and getting coy whenever Ros mentioned riding without irons, rather than saying she wasn't so game to do that anymore.

This, of course, is the piece people often "forget" to do. It's easier to look for a problem's source outside. Turning the periscope inward to discover our role in something? Just another sign of having grown up.

MOM LIKES WINNING TOO MUCH

Dear Janet: I have a problem I've been too embarrassed to ask anyone about, but it's sticking in my craw.

My daughter has been competitive in combined training for the past few years and is now winning on two horses at Preliminary. Twice now, a different parent has mentioned something in passing to me about how much I seem to get out of my daughter's winning. At first I took it as a light joke, but after the second time I started to wonder.

I do get excited when Beth does well, and I have to admit I'm bummed when things go poorly. I don't think I get inappropriate or anything, but somehow it's hard to tell by myself. (I'm widowed, so I don't have Beth's father to bounce ideas off.) I'm wondering, though, if her winning has become more important to me than it should be. Can you help? —Sue

Sue, if only more parents were as responsive as you to the cues they get from the people sharing their world! Anyone can get away with dismissing a comment once, but you're smart to pay attention when you get the same one twice. Maybe people notice that your moods change too much depending upon how well Beth is doing, or that you get agitated and short with others prior to events. Maybe they see Beth straining under an invisible pressure to please you. Maybe anything. Ask yourself the following questions, Sue, and see what ideas you come up with for the feedback you're getting.

• **Have I been taking my daughter's wins and losses personally—as if they reflect on my own athletic ability, or my mothering?** Remember how important it is that parents separate their children's achievements from their own. Pride and propriety are two different things. And as far as mothering goes, Beth can fall flat on her face, but the way you pick her up will speak volumes about the kind of mom you are.

• **Have my daughter and I been arguing more about her riding? Have we begun to feel more like adversaries than teammates? Have I developed more aggressive goals than she has?** Make sure Beth is the one leading this dance. If it doesn't remain her choice to go on, it won't remain her passion, either.

• **Do I ever find myself feeling angry at my daughter when she doesn't do as well as I expected?** You know better so pull your punches. Besides, anybody who's in this sport is always doing the best she can at the time. I've yet to meet a rider who didn't try her hardest when she really wanted it.

• **Am I urging her on to more events, lessons, and clinics than she wants to go to?** Ask Beth directly about this one. If she says you are, find out from her how much training she does want. If it's less than you think she needs to compete safely at her current level, discuss with her what you feel are the base requirements—and get professional input as well. If it's less than you think she needs to advance, discuss with her why she doesn't wish to press on at this time—and respect her answer.

• **Do I enjoy bragging to others about my daughter's accomplishments? Do I embarrass her by what I say?** That you would want to brag is understandable—but save it for grandma, close friends, your daughter herself. And ask Beth if there are pet phrases you use that she'd rather you not say. They might seem benign to you but make her uncomfortable.

Sue, don't ever take any of this to mean you can't be a tremendous fan of your daughter's riding. You can be Beth's biggest fan and enjoy her victories gloriously and still never give the impression that her winning means more to you than her playing a good game and loving it. Let her enthusiasm, and her hunger to compete and win, be the engine for your team—and let her own words to you be your guide as to how big of a push she wants, if any.

And, Sue, just a thought, but—how about taking those ribbons off your ponytail? They're a dead giveaway. Kidding!

GOT A NON-HORSEY PARENT?

Dear Janet: Even though I've been riding for seven years, my parents seem to have no interest in learning more about the sport. I want to progress in the horse world, but without their help I feel as if I'll be stuck in the same hunter classes forever! I'm really interested in combined training and dressage, but I'm beginning to doubt I'll ever get to do those activities. Any suggestions? —Diane

Diane, I often hear from teenagers disappointed in their parents' lack of enthusiasm for horses and riding. Let me try to help you discover some ways to promote your parents' support for your riding without your seeming pushy or presumptuous. First . . .

Help your parents understand the culture of horses.

If your parents didn't grow up around horses or riding, they may have difficulty appreciating what all the fuss is about. They may still think of horses as "farm" animals—or as "pets for the privileged." They may not see where horses fit in an urban or suburban lifestyle, for instance, or what value the care and riding of horses can have for you as a young person. Why not help them better understand that value by asking yourself to identify one way you think your involvement with horses has made you a better person (i.e., more responsible, confident, self-aware), then writing your parents a note or poem about it?

Help them see the appeal of a different discipline.

You and your folks apparently have been making the rounds of hunter shows as your interests are changing toward eventing. Switching to a new discipline, with its different language, clothing, and culture, can be harder than moving to a new country. Try taking your parents to a horse trial or Pony Club rally where they can see combined training firsthand. Say to them, "Guys, I want to show you some things I'd like to do with my horse.

It looks like a lot of fun. There's a horse trial this Saturday in Smithtown. Can we walk around and I'll show you what I'm talking about?"

Keep in mind, too, Diane, that they might be worried about the new activities bringing new costs. If you think that's a factor, be prepared to give them some idea of what expenses (new equipment or tack, additional training?) might be involved.

When you're at the rally or trial, explain to your folks how dressage and cross-country and stadium jumping are different from what you do now (to the non-rider, it can all look alike!) and why they appeal to you more. It's also possible your parents have made some social connections at the shows you've been attending and are reluctant to start up with a whole new circle of people. Meeting friendly, chatty parents with kids involved in CT could help.

Respond to concerns for your safety.

Everybody knows what happened to Christopher Reeve—and, like it or not, that's the first thing many people think of when they hear "combined training" or "eventing." Ask your parents if their reluctance is safety-related. Say, "You know, I've wanted to try some cross-country riding, but you don't seem so keen on the idea. Do you worry about me doing these new things?" If they say yes, tell them the specific things CT riders do to be safe. Show them the safety equipment (vests, headgear) in catalogues, describe the graduated levels of training and competition, and discuss with them how you'd go about making sure you were being properly trained.

In all fairness to the scores of parents baffled by a child's seeming obsession with horses, getting one's bearings in the horse world can be tough—especially coming in as an adult. Adding to parents' mystification is the ease with which children move and work around these animals whose one misstep can crush a foot. Parents need help comprehending the emotional and psychological pull of horses, so their puzzlement or intimidation can get replaced by curiosity. Only then will they begin to understand why the same daughter who refuses to wear the same pajamas two nights in a row happily spends her day in clothes covered with green slobber and horse poop.

ABOUT THE AUTHOR

D r. Janet Sasson Edgette is an equestrian sport psychologist based in the western suburbs of Philadelphia as well as a nationally recognized specialist in the area of adolescent and family counseling. She is the author of **Heads Up!: Practical Sports Psychology for Riders, Their Families, and Their Trainers** and three additional books about counseling and parenting teenagers. From 1995 through 2003, Janet wrote her "Heads Up" column for *Practical Horseman* magazine and served for much of that time as *PH*'s consulting sport psychologist. Her work has also been featured in *Horse & Rider, Hunter & Sport Horse, The Morgan Horse, Quarter Horse Journal, HoofPrint, Horse Show, The Paint Horse,* and other equestrian publications.

Janet travels frequently throughout the United States speaking about the psychological aspects of being involved with horses and conducting interactive, educational seminars for competitive and recreational riders, instructors, and the parents of young riders. She has spent the last fifteen years developing a philosophy of performance enhancement that departs from traditional notions of relaxation and imagery in favor of a simpler, less effortful approach. This approach helps riders to find room for their competition nerves or intruding doubts while learning how to ride well in spite of them. By handling unpleasant or unwanted emotions as such, the rider can avoid much of the stress about trying to "make" them go away and can become freer to ride. Paradoxically, this is exactly the formula for getting these feelings to recede into the background anyway, and to begin to dissipate quietly on their own.

Janet started riding during childhood. In her teens, she became a student of legendary horseman Wayne Carroll and his father, Frank Carroll, at Secor Farms in White Plains, New York. She spent her junior years competing successfully in the equitation, hunter, and jumper divisions and rode several times in both the ASPCA Maclay and AHSA Medal finals, including work-offs for each. Janet returned to the show ring as an adult and gravitated quickly to the jumpers—where, under the tutelage of George Morris, she remained competitive at such shows as the American Gold Cup, Upperville, and the Winter Equestrian Festival in Tampa. She continues to compete while maintaining her private practice and speaking schedule and, along with her husband, John, raising three young boys.